Praise for *Faith and Politics*

"...k is an important contribution to understanding one of the greatest ...n world affairs and demonstrates why Nigeria—because of its ...ces with democratic federalism and building alliances across religious ...no-regional lines can provide important models for other nations facing ...hallenges."

...ard A. Joseph, Northwestern University

". Paden brings over forty years of deep experience in Nigeria to this masterful ... which argues that this incredibly complex nation deserves a central role in ...trategy on how to engage the Muslim world. He contends that Nigeria has ...jue global role to play as both a potential model for inter-religious political ...mmodation and as a potential bridging player in global politics between the ...an-dominated West and the Muslim world."

...rren Kew, University of Massachusetts, Boston

"...n, America's foremost expert on Islam in Nigeria, provides an analysis of ...Nigeria, with substantial Muslim and Christian populations, has mastered ...isk of keeping the country together. The author delves into the formal ...informal federalism arrangements, the role of religious leadership, and the ...rstandings about power sharing that explain this success while providing sound ...nmendations for what Nigeria must do to preserve this coexistence. This book ... outstanding contribution to our understanding of nation building."

...nceton N. Lyman, Council on Foreign Relations

Faith and Politics in Nigeria

Faith and Politics in Nigeria

NIGERIA
AS A
PIVOTAL
STATE
IN THE
MUSLIM
WORLD

John N. Paden

UNITED STATES INSTITUTE OF PEACE PRESS

Washington, D.C.

UNITED STATES INSTITUTE OF PEACE
1200 17th Street NW, Suite 200
Washington, DC 20036-3011
www.usip.org

First published 2008

Printed in the United States of America

The paper used in this publication meets the minimum requirements of American National Standards for Information Science—Permanence of Paper for Printed Library Materials, ANSI Z39.48-1984.

Library of Congress Cataloging-in-Publication Data

Paden, John N.
    Faith and politics in Nigeria : Nigeria as a pivotal state in the
  Muslim world / by John N. Paden.
        p. cm.
    Includes bibliographical references and index.
    ISBN 978-1-60127-029-0 (pbk. : alk. paper)
    1. Nigeria--Politics and government. 2. Nigeria--Foreign relations.
3. Religion and politics--Nigeria. 4. Political culture--Nigeria--Religious
aspects. 5. Islamic countries--Relations--Nigeria. 6. Nigeria--Relations--
Islamic countries. 7. Islam and state--Nigeria. 8. Nigeria--Ethnic
relations. 9. Islam--Relations--Christianity--Nigeria. I. Title.

    DT515.59.P35 2007
    966.905′4--dc22
                        2007044241

This book is dedicated to the unity of Nigeria.

Contents

Illustrations

Foreword

In this slim and readable volume, John Paden draws on more than forty years experience living and teaching in Nigeria to examine how Nigeria fits into the emerging global context. With its population of more than 140 million and vast oil reserves, Nigeria maintains a dominant presence in Africa and holds a significance that extends well beyond the continent's borders. But Nigeria's regional and international import is derived not just from its sheer size and natural resources. It is also derived from its unique demographic composition: it has the largest concentration of Muslims west of the Persian Gulf and is by far the largest country in the world with an approximate demographic balance between Muslims and Christians. As Paden argues herein, if nothing else, the manner in which Nigeria manages its demographic diversity makes it a pivotal state both within the Muslim world and within the larger international community.

Recalling his earlier highly noteworthy research on northern history, culture, religion, and politics, Paden states that the key to understanding Islam in Nigeria—and therefore the place of Nigeria in the Muslim world—is to recognize the centrality of the Sokoto Caliphate. Indeed, history is a living presence in Nigeria. The Sokoto Caliphate, founded in the early nineteenth century by Usman Dan Fodio, continues to exert strong cultural influence in Nigeria and West Africa. Dan Fodio emphasized "justice"—including the removal of unfair taxes—and the need for Islamic education as a guide for the community. During the British colonial period in the north (1903–60), this caliphal system, including sharia law, was retained as the basis of colonial rule and there has been a continuous attempt to interpret this legacy by northern political and religious leaders ever since.

Paden argues that not only is the Sokoto Caliphate one of the largest precolonial political systems in sub-Saharan Africa but that it has also been part of the direct experience of fourteen of the thirty-six contemporary states in Nigeria. Furthermore, historical resistance to the caliphate has been part of the legacy of two additional northern Muslim states: Yobe and Borno. Three other states in the Middle Belt were part of the former Northern Region and are integral to the northern political scene. Thus, nineteen of the thirty-six Nigerian states are part of the former Northern Region. Additionally, in the southwest region, several Yoruba states identified with resistance to the Sokoto Caliphate in the nineteenth century, although Ilorin (in the north) is predominantly Yoruba. At present, the southwest is demographically about half Muslim and has a complex and unique relationship with the north.

After the return to civilian rule in 1999, twelve of the far-northern states returned to forms of sharia law—in criminal and civil domains. As Paden states, this was seen as a controversial move in the north and among the country's various Christian communities (although non-Muslims are not subject to Islamic law). He argues that the sharia "issue" has since "normalized," that is was a nonissue in the 2003 and 2007 elections, and that it is unlikely to rear its head in the near future.

Paden also focuses on ethnoreligious balancing mechanisms within Nigeria, such as the power shift from the southwest to the north in the 2007 election. He notes that all three major candidates for president in the April 2007 elections were from caliphal states: Umaru Yar'Adua and Muhammadu Buhari from the "balancing state" of Katsina and Atiku Abubakar from Adamawa, which borders non-Muslim/indigenous lands. While Yar'Adua prevailed in the flawed election, the tone was set in many ways by Buhari, who, as leader of the major opposition party, emphasized the need for justice in the fight against corruption and education in the fight against poverty. His popularity at the grassroots level in the north was eclipsed by the power of the incumbent party, but subsequent court challenges to this election emphasize the "legal" tradition that is very much part of the northern/Islamic legacy.

Paden also details how in recent years the various major factions and geographic centers of the Muslim community in Nigeria have come together under the Nigerian Supreme Council for Islamic Affairs (NSCIA). (Its president is the Sultan of Sokoto, its vice president is the Shehu of Borno, and its secretary-general is a distinguished Yoruba legal scholar.) This "big tent" tries to be inclusive of Sufis, legalists, and traditional emirate authorities and of the obvious geographical nodes and networks: the caliphate states, Borno, and the Yoruba states. Although NSCIA is clearly an "establishment" organization, it has nonetheless occasionally acted in support of the radical elements in the north, such as during the debate on the polio vaccination issue. Paden also profiles two "outsider" groups that have challenged this establishment in the north, that is, the so-called Shiites and the so-called Taliban, both relatively small groups.

But the larger issue of Muslim-Christian relations is the theme of this volume, including the mechanisms, both constitutional and cultural, that have encouraged national harmony through a "people-of-the-book" approach. For example, the country's recent census did not include questions on religious or ethnic identity; the major political parties tend to balance their national tickets between north and south; ethnoreligious labeling of political parties is not acceptable; there is a presumed "power shift" or rotation of presidential power between northern and southern candidates; zonal or geographical surrogate identities are utilized to blur religious and ethnic identities; "federal character" principles in the constitution require a power-sharing approach to all federal executive appointments, including the cabinet; media coverage of sensitive religious issues and conflict increasingly demonstrates an awareness of the need "not to cry fire in a crowded religious theater"; the national budget—funded largely by oil income—is shared among the states on revenue-sharing principles; a new federal capital has been built in Abuja to give proximate access to the six geographic zones; a national interreligious council has been established with twenty-five Muslim leaders and twenty-five Christian leaders—cochaired by the president of the Christian Association of Nigeria (CAN) and the president of the NSCIA—that deals with interfaith relations at all levels.

Within the larger Nigerian context, Paden concludes that this balancing of ethnoreligious and regional diversity poses five challenges of nation building: (1) establishing a workable political system; (2) consolidating rule of law; (3) developing capacities for conflict resolution; (4) facilitating economic development; and (5) stemming corruption at all levels. He calls for a democratic federalism approach in meeting these challenges.

At the international level, Paden focuses on Nigeria's role in West Africa, especially in the Economic Community of West African States (ECOWAS); in the broader African context, through the African Union; and in numerous international organizations. He examines the special relationship of Nigerian Muslims—who are almost entirely Sunni—with Saudi Arabia, both on a diplomatic and spiritual level. Yet the sensitive Muslim-Christian balance also relates to Nigeria's ambiguous role in the Organization of the Islamic Conference (OIC).

Finally, Paden assesses the special challenge of improving U.S. relations with Nigeria's Muslim community. In today's world, what are the challenges of U.S. engagement with Nigeria in terms of military and security relations; diplomatic and political relations; economic, business, and educational relations; and cultural, religious, and nongovernmental relations? Paden argues that the United States needs to engage and normalize its relations with Nigeria at all levels, especially in the Northern States. It must not be pulled into the trap of relying on political actors in Abuja (or in the diaspora) to target "evil doers," who are, in most cases, legitimate opposition leaders. He further cautions: do not allow the obvious needs of the oil industry to "wag the dog" and dominate all relations between the United States and Nigeria. Do not let the global war on terrorism poison relations with the 99 percent of Nigerian Muslims who are moderate and generally friendly to the United States. Come to grips with the need for a deeper understanding of Islam in West Africa, especially in Nigeria. Finally, he advises that the United States should set an example of tolerance between people of the book at home and abroad.

Overall, this volume will be of deep interest to Nigerians, Africans, and the broader international community. Once again, Paden has contributed to our understanding of a complicated, multilevel drama as Nigerian Muslims search for their position in the global arena and, at the same time, work to set a positive example with their Christian countrymen. I strongly recommend this book to scholars, diplomats, and public-policy practitioners.

—Ambassador Ibrahim Gambari

A Nigerian scholar and diplomat, Ambassador Ibrahim Gambari is the current undersecretary-general of the United Nations for the Department of Political Affairs and special adviser on Africa. He formerly served as Nigeria's Minister of External Affairs and Nigeria's Permanent Representative to the United Nations and taught at Ahmadu Bello University/ABU and the Johns Hopkins School of Advanced International Studies.

Faith and Politics in Nigeria

1

Introduction: Nigeria in Global Perspective

With a population of more than 140 million, Nigeria is the most populous country in Africa. It is the fourth largest member of the Organization of the Islamic Conference (OIC), after Indonesia, Pakistan, and Bangladesh, and, with Turkey and Iran, has the sixth largest number of Muslims in the world. Only Indonesia, Pakistan, India, Bangladesh, and Egypt have larger Muslim populations. Most important, it stands as the largest country with an approximate balance between its Muslim and Christian populations. Nigeria's ethnolinguistic and religious diversity make it one of the most complex countries in the world, and it is the need to accommodate these many strands that has been the driving force in the country since its independence in 1960, and especially since the civil war of 1967–70.

Nigeria is the seventh largest oil producer in the world. With the price of oil hovering between $40 and $98 per barrel between 2004 and 2007, the windfall profits to Nigeria have been considerable. As of June 2007, Nigeria had well over $48 billion in the international banking system after having paid off its $12 billion discounted debt to the Paris Club. These reserves are over and above its recurrent budget allocations. In turn, this oil-boom phenomenon has affected Nigerian politics in fundamental ways.

Since returning to civilian rule in 1999, after fifteen years of martial rule, Nigeria has conducted a major experiment in democratic federalism through its thirty-six states and 774 local government areas. With the two-term limit of the administration of Olusegun Obasanjo expiring, the elections in spring 2007 were critical to a civilian-to-civilian transition in a volatile political environment. In 2000, the twelve far-northern governors had reintroduced sharia law in the criminal domain in their states, which are largely Muslim. The Nigerian Christian community, largely in the south and the middle belt, worried about the implication for the future of Nigeria. But much of this tension has lessened in the seven years since. This is partly due to the "national unity" and "Nigeria is one" approach that all political parties have tried to adopt, working across regional and religious cleavages in national coalitions.

Nigeria is probably the least well known of the Muslim world's pivotal states. Its role as the dominant African state, its extraordinary influence in West Africa, its significance as a major world oil producer, and its experience with democratic rule since 1999 make Nigeria a critical country, especially in its relations with the United States.

Organization of the Chapters

The author's experiences in Nigeria over the past four decades have contributed to general observations throughout this volume. Because this is an interpretative essay, an effort has been made to avoid extensive footnotes, except to denote referenced sources and, in some cases, to provide illustrative background detail.

This first chapter provides an overview of Nigeria, focusing on its comparative position within the Muslim world, and includes brief sketches of the following subjects to provide the foundational context: demographics, religion, and ethnicity; urbanization and education; oil, agriculture, and industry; income distribution and links to the global economy; and national and military politics.

Chapter 2 delves into the sources of Nigerian influence and significance. These include more detail on the idea of Nigeria as a pivotal state in the Muslim world, especially in relation to other Muslim states. The argument is made that Nigeria's distinctiveness revolves around its nearly equal demographic divide between Muslims and Christians. The Nigerian model of "federal character" is outlined, which balances the national demographics through representation in the executive branches. The concept of cooperation among "people of the book"—particularly between Muslims and Christians—is also articulated. Finally, Nigeria's key role in Africa and in the world is explored.

Chapter 2 also explores Muslim organizations in Nigeria, including the Muslim Sufi brotherhoods and Izala, student and youth organizations, women's organizations, national umbrella organizations, and antiestablishment networks, such as groups identified as "Shiites" and "Taliban" but whose real orientations are unclear. Finally, Nigerian links to transnational systems in Africa and beyond are discussed—for instance, nonstate and state-sector links—as well as issues of international security and economic development.

Chapter 3 discusses the challenges of nation building in Nigeria, including establishing a workable political system, consolidating rule of law, developing capacities for conflict resolution, facilitating economic development, and stemming corruption at all levels.

Chapter 4 explores pathways of change, including the politics of alternative futures for Nigeria—for example, the Shell Oil "Vision 2010" projections for Nigeria and certain worst-case scenarios—and looks at power sharing and the power-shifting aspects of the country's 2007 election. It also explores pathways of political change, such as partition, centralization, and democratic federalism.

Chapter 5 assesses four dimensions of U.S. engagement with Nigeria. These include military and security relations; diplomatic and political relations; economic, business, and educational relations; and cultural, religious, and non-governmental organization (NGO) relations. In addition, some suggestions are offered on the future of U.S. relations with Nigeria.

The last chapter evaluates Nigeria's role as a pivotal Muslim state.

Profiles of Nigeria

While hard data on socioeconomic patterns in Nigeria have always been difficult to establish, various statistical estimates are available. Where possible, U.S. government public data are used in this overview, supplemented by the author's best judgment.

Demographics, Religion, and Ethnicity

The most recent census in Nigeria was held on March 21–28, 2006, but the release of the census results was postponed at least twice by the National Population Commission (NPC).[1] Finally, in the run-up to the 2007 national elections, the commission announced the results. With a total population of 140,003,542, there are 71,709,859 men and 68,293,683 women in the country. According to this census data, an estimated 42.3 percent of Nigeria's population is aged 0–14 years, 54.6 percent 15–64 years, and 3.1 percent 65 years and older. The population growth is estimated at 2.38 percent each year and the median age is 18.7 years old. The estimated total fertility rate (average number of children per woman) is 5.49. The census estimates life expectancy to be 47.08 years, although the World Bank estimates this to be 45.3 years. The census also showed that Kano State in the far north has the largest number of people (see table 1).

The 2006 census, as per Nigeria's last census in 1991, did not ask questions about ethnicity or religion. These are still sensitive questions in a country that has a strong history of geocultural regionalism and religious diversity. This sensitivity is reflected in the political tensions that have surrounded every census since independence in 1960.[2]

Prior to the release of the 2006 census data, the 1991 census had been widely used as the basis for recent population-related estimates and projections. For example, U.S. government estimates put the population of Nigeria in July

---

1. For background, see National Population Commision, *NPC News* 5, no. 3 (September 2006). Also see National Population Commission, *State Forum for Stakeholders on the Status of 2006 Census* (November 2006).

2. See "Census Provisional Result Out October, says NPC Chairman," *ThisDay*, April 20, 2006; "Census 2006: Just How Many Heads Were Missing?" *Vanguard*, March 26, 2006; "Census: Kano Fears Citizens May Lose Rights," *Daily Triumph*, March 24, 2006; and "60,000 Police to Monitor Census in Katsina," *Daily Triumph*, March 21, 2006.

TABLE 1   PROVISIONAL POPULATION TOTAL CENSUS, 2006

State	Persons	State	Persons
Abia	2,833,909	Kano	9,383,682
Adamawa	3,168,101	Katsina	5,792,578
Akwa-Ibom	3,920,208	Kebbi	n/a
Anambra	n/a	Kogi	3,278,487
Bauchi	4,676,465	Kwara	2,371,089
Bayelsa	1,703,358	Lagos	9,013,534
Benue	4,219,244	Nasarawa	1,863,275
Borno	4,151,193	Niger	3,950,249
Cross River	2,888,966	Ogun	3,728,098
Delta	4,098,391	Ondo	3,441,024
Ebonyi	2,173,501	Osun	3,423,535
Edo	3,218,332	Oyo	5,591,589
Ekiti	2,384,212	Plateau	3,178,712
Enugu	3,257,298	Rivers	5,185,400
FCT Abuja	1,404,201	Sokoto	3,696,999
Gombe	2,353,879	Taraba	2,300,736
Imo	3,934,899	Yobe	2,321,591
Jigawa	4,348,649	Zamfara	3,259,846
Kaduna	6,066,562	**Total**	**140,003,542**

Source: *Nigeria Factbook* (Kaduna: Risafu and Company, 2007).

2004 at 137 million. At an estimated 2.45 percent growth rate, the July 2005 estimate was 140.36 million, and the July 2006 estimate was 144 million. In 2005, the Nigerian ambassador to the United States, reflecting the views of President Obasanjo, estimated the population at 150 million, while the World Bank estimated it to be around 137 million.[3] In short, although there have been a wide range of population estimates, the prevailing data indicate between 140 and 150 million as of 2007. Much of the controversy inside Nigeria regarding census data has to do with balance of populations between the thirty-six states (see map 1).

Other basic statistics include these: in 2003, only 9 percent of Nigerian women used modern contraceptives, although 35 percent of women wanted to space or postpone pregnancies, according to the United States Agency for International Development (USAID). Also, in 2003 an estimated 5.8 percent of the population was HIV/AIDS positive, resulting in an estimated 310,000

---

3. Nigerian ambassador to the United States George Obiozor, in an interview with *Washington Diplomat* (August 2006, 15), said, Nigeria's "actual population is around 150 million, which would rank it number six after China, India, the United States, Indonesia, and Brazil. Because of extremely high growth rates—its population exploded by 33 percent between 1990 and 2000—Nigeria is now ahead of Russia, Pakistan, Bangladesh, Japan, and Mexico."

deaths. According to Nigerian media reports, this percentage may have come down slightly. In 2005, for example, the official figure was at 4.4 percent.

Nigeria has a large population with high rates of growth and a youth bulge approaching adulthood. The incidence of disease vectors in Nigeria, as elsewhere, puts an enormous burden on the country's healthy productive population. Health concerns are a major factor in the increase in Christian "health and wealth" churches, as well as in many of the local Muslim communities.

Regarding religious and ethnic identities, U.S. government and authoritative Nigerian estimates put the number of Muslims at 50 percent, Christians at 40 percent, and indigenous-belief followers at 10 percent.[4] In practice, as noted, it is widely recognized that the country is about half Muslim and half Christian, with pockets of traditional ethnic and local religions in both Muslim and Christian geocultural zones. Estimates of the number of ethnolinguistic groups in Nigeria range between 250 and 400, depending on how dialects and subgroups are counted. Yet, three major ethnolinguistic clusters predominate: Hausa and Fulani (29 percent) in the north; Yoruba (21 percent) in the southwest; and Igbo (18 percent) in the southeast. Thus, these three identity groups constitute about 68 percent of the national population. In addition, there are a number of midsized ethnolinguistic groups: Ijaw (10 percent) in the south-south; Kanuri (4 percent) in the northeast; Ibibio (3.5 percent), also in the south-south; and Tiv (2.5 percent) in the Middle Belt. There are dozens (if not hundreds) of smaller groups, especially in the Middle Belt and south-south areas. English is the official national language, with Hausa, Yoruba, and Igbo designated as national languages for certain purposes.

There are six semiofficial geocultural zones in Nigeria, three each in the northern and southern regions of the country. Muslim populations reside mainly in the north and southwest. In the north (including the northwest, north-central, and northeast), the emirate states were part of the nineteenth-century Sokoto caliphate (see map 2). The Borno environs (including Borno and Yobe) in the northeast have been Muslim since about the eleventh century. The Middle Belt (in the north-central zone) is a mixture of Christian and Muslim populations.

The Yoruba-speaking communities in the southwest are about half Muslim and half Christian. The south-south minority areas and the Igbo-speaking areas in the southeast are predominantly Christian. It is sometimes argued that the "north" is predominantly Muslim and the "south" predominantly

---

4. See *Nigeria Factbook* (Kaduna: Risafu and Company, 2007), 7.

Map 1   Nigeria and Its Thirty-Six States

Christian, but this pattern is blurred by the mixed religious populations in the Middle Belt and southwest.[5]

The intensity of religious identity in Nigeria is regarded as one of the highest in the world.[6] Much of this intensity developed during the military period (1984–99) but appears to have increased during the Fourth Republic (1999–present). Thus, multireligious diversity in Nigeria now has a force that impacts politics profoundly and is very much in the international public eye.[7]

Urbanization and Education

The oil boom caused a major shift of populations from the countryside to the cities. Since the 1970s, Nigeria has had one of the highest urbanization rates in the world. The former capital in the southwest, Lagos, is a major port, and although the 2006 census puts the population there at around 9 million, the governor has protested this figure. Some observers maintain that the population of the greater metropolitan area is as high as 16 million! Between 1970 and about 1995, the population of Lagos doubled every ten years, until the capital was finally shifted to Abuja in the mid-1990s.

The Federal Capital Territory (FCT) at Abuja was designed in the late 1970s as the geographic center of the country, that is, with equal access to all geocultural zones. Because of the high incidence of river blindness, now eradicated, the area selected in the 1970s was virtually uninhabited. Today, with oil revenues and global technologies, Abuja has become one of the most modern cities in sub-Saharan Africa and by 2006 had a population of 1.4 million, according to the 2006 census. The FCT minister, however, estimated the population to be as high as 7 million in 2006, perhaps reflecting the transient

---

5. For details, see John N. Paden, *Muslim Civic Cultures and Conflict Resolution: The Challenge of Democratic Federalism in Nigeria* (Washington, D.C.: Brookings Institution Press, 2005).

6. See BBC News, *World Edition*, February 26, 2004. Surveys by the BBC were done in the United States, the United Kingdom, Israel, India, South Korea, Indonesia, Nigeria, Russia, Mexico, and Lebanon and concluded, "Nigeria is the most religious country in the world."

    For a Nigerian perspective on this pattern, see Sabella Ogbobode Abidde, "The Destruction of Nigeria by Religious Means" (www.gamji.com, accessed December 8, 2005). Abidde notes, "I have always felt that the destruction of Nigeria would come by way of one or a combination of the following cleavages: ethnic and religious conflicts, cataclysms with origin in the Niger Delta, or the combustion of pent-up anger within the military. Lately, however, a fourth dimension seems to be manifesting itself within the Nigerian fault line: the religionization of Nigeria." He goes on to say that "churches have become as 'common as fast-food joints' and that the born-again are everywhere, all claiming to be God's children, all claiming to be the chosen ones. There are more born-again in Nigeria than the United States, United Kingdom, and Canada combined. There are more born-again in Nigerian prisons than in all the prisons of the Western world combined. Active villains are born again; active prostitutes are born again; active armed-robbers are born again; cheats and vagabonds and everything and everybody in between are born again. . . . That's Nigerian-style religion for you. . . . Prior to the 2003 Nigerian elections, President Olusegun Obasanjo was asked whether he was going to contest the elections. His answer had a fantastic and fatalistic tone. He said, 'The decision will be made by God' and 'Whatever God decides, you can be assured that I will abide by him.'"

7. "In God's Name," *Economist*, November 3, 2007, 3ff.

MAP 2   SOKOTO CALIPHATE IN THE NINETEENTH CENTURY

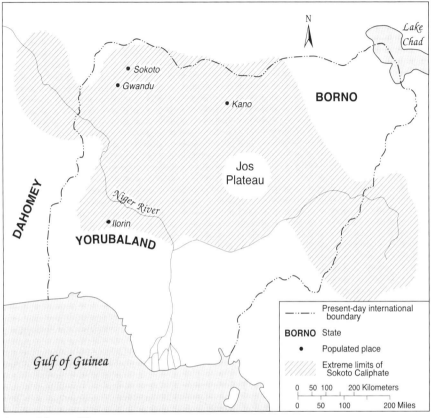

Source: Library of Congress.

nature of some inhabitants, who may have returned to their original states during the census. Other major cities with populations well over a million include metropolitan Kano (which the governor estimates as high as 12 million) and Kaduna in the north, Ibadan in the southwest, Onitsha and Nsukka in the southeast, and Port Harcourt in the south-south.

Regarding education, the national oil economy has made possible an extensive system of primary, secondary, and university education, including an increasing number of private universities, although there are regional variations.[8] According to Nigerian estimates, 68 percent of the population (age

8. See the editorial, "Application for More Private Universities," *Guardian* (Lagos), May 16, 2006, which reported on the current initiatives of forty-five individuals or groups interested in increasing the number of universities beyond the current seventy-four run by the federal government (26), the states (26), and the private sector (16). "Most of these universities are located south of the Niger (River), with a high concentration in the Southwest. Certainly this has implications for the future manpower production in the country." For discussion of a new northern university, Katsina State Islamic University, see "Katsina State Varsity'll Be Great Says Dantata," *Daily Triumph*, November 9, 2007.

15 and over) is literate, with rates of 75.7 percent for males and 60.6 percent for females (2003 estimate).[9] Adult education facilities are also widespread. However, funding for teachers, especially high-quality teachers, is always in short supply. Many educational facilities are in critical need of maintenance and repairs. About a million candidates took the national university entrance exam for the 2005–06 session, but the universities could only accommodate about two hundred thousand of them.[10] Private universities may take up part of the slack, but disappointed postsecondary students will have an impact on political and even religious movements.

The Nigerian estimate for secondary school attendance is 32 percent for males and 27 percent for females. At secondary and university levels, all instruction is in English. In addition, the predominantly Muslim areas, especially in the north, have parallel systems of Koranic schools and higher Islamic schools (Islamiyya), in which the language of learning is vernacular (for example, Hausa) and the subject matter is in Arabic. Islamiyya schools may try to blend Western and Islamic knowledge. The number of Islamic schools in a Muslim population center such as Kano may be as high as twenty thousand.

Oil, Agriculture, and Industry

Crude oil production accounts for 90–95 percent of Nigerian export revenues, over 90 percent of foreign exchange earnings, and 80 percent of government revenues. In June 2004 crude oil production averaged 2.14 million barrels per day. Deepwater exploration began in 2005 in the Gulf of Guinea, and Nigeria expects to produce 4.5 million barrels per day by 2010. Nigerian oil reserve estimates range from 25 billion to 35 billion barrels. In 2004–07, with the price of a barrel of oil moving from about $40 per barrel to about $98 per barrel, enormous windfall revenues have accrued to the Nigerian government, which had projected budgets based on an average of $23 per barrel in 2004 to around $32 per barrel in 2005 and $40 per barrel in 2007. Nigerian officials estimated the surplus to be in the $20-billion range for the first nine months of 2004 alone, and they have further increased since 2005. As noted previously, after Nigeria paid off its international debt in April 2006, it had about $48 billion of its budget in its "excess crude account" of international reserves.[11]

---

9. *Nigeria Factbook*, 7.

10. *Guardian*, "Application for More Private Universities."

11. See "Nigeria in Deal to Pay off Most of Its Foreign Debt," *New York Times*, October 21, 2005. See also "Nigeria Pays off Its Big Debt, Sign of an Economic Rebound," *New York Times*, April 22, 2006. Thus, "Nigeria reached a deal last October with the Paris Club, which includes the United States, Germany, France and other wealthy nations, that allowed it to pay off about $30 billion in accumulated debt for about $12 billion, an overall discount of about 60%." For a Nigerian perspective, see "Excess Crude Earning Hits N1.4 Trillion," *Guardian* (Lagos), September 6, 2005. As of 2007, the official exchange rate between the Nigerian naira and the U.S. dollar was N126 = US$1.

Joint ventures account for 95 percent of Nigeria's crude oil production, and Shell Oil produces 50 percent of all oil. The Nigerian National Petroleum Corporation (NNPC) has a 55 percent stake in Shell's operations and a 60 percent stake in ExxonMobil, ChevronTexaco, ConocoPhillips, Eni S.p.A, and Total S.A. In 2003 the United States received 838,000 barrels of Nigerian oil per day, making Nigeria the fifth largest oil exporter to the U.S. and supplying about 8.7 percent of all U.S. imported oil. Almost all crude oil is produced in the south-south (Niger Delta) coastal zone of Nigeria. Subsequently, since 2003, about one-fifth of Nigerian oil has been taken off stream because of insurgency violence in the Delta.

Regarding agriculture and industry, the ecology of Nigeria includes two major zones: the savanna lands in the north and the rain forest zones in the south. In the north, grain crops such as millet and sorghum, plus root crops such as cassava, provide the backbone of the local economies. (The shortfall of rain in 2007 produced much local concern.) Peanuts ("groundnuts") used to be the main export crop from the north, but during the oil-economy era, this crop has been eclipsed. Cattle herding, plus sheep and goats, provide the main elements of animal husbandry. Hides and skins provide a significant export.

In the south, yams are a staple and there are cash crops such as cocoa, palm oil, rice, rubber, and timber. In general, large animals do not thrive in the south because of disease vectors (especially sleeping sickness), and there is a dependence on northern livestock production. Fishing provides a stable protein in many local coastal or river communities. Industries have developed in virtually every Nigerian urban area, often fueled by oil money. The construction industry has been especially active. However, cheap imports (both legal and smuggled), especially from China, have put many Nigerian light industries (including textiles) out of business.

Income Distribution and Links to the Global Economy

The U.S. estimate for Nigerian per capita income in 2002 was $290. USAID estimates that 60–70 percent of Nigerians live on less than one dollar per day. While the estimated real growth rate of gross domestic product (GDP) has been a healthy 7.1 percent, there has been an increasing gap between those who are linked to the national oil economy—including a wide range of government projects—and those who are living at local or subsistence levels. Government privatization programs, that is, the sale of previously state-owned assets, have tended to benefit those who have government or senior corporate connections.

Regarding links to the international economy, as of 2005 Nigerian external debt was around $31 billion. The Nigerian government has negotiated debt relief, but in light of high oil prices and the extraordinary needs of non-energy-producing African countries, there has been little international receptivity to outright debt cancellation. Most debt was owed to the European-based Paris Club, with a very small portion to the United States. As noted, the Paris Club debt was renegotiated or written down in 2005, and by early 2006 the entire amount was paid off for the discounted sum of about $12 billion.

After these Paris Club negotiations, the Nigerian government hoped to remain debt free by requiring all crude oil producers to refine 50 percent or more of all oil produced inside Nigeria by 2006. But this requirement did not move forward, and none of the oil majors is building refineries or seeking to purchase refineries that the government is trying to privatize.[12] Prior to the 2007 election, President Obasanjo sold two major refineries, one in Kaduna and one in Port Harcourt, to wealthy political supporters. (This was subsequently reversed after the election.)[13]

Nigeria's major export partners include the United States (38.3 percent), India (9.9 percent), Brazil (6.8 percent), Spain (6.2 percent), France (5.6 percent), and Japan (4 percent). Nigeria's major import partners include the United States (15.6 percent), the United Kingdom (9.6 percent), Germany (7.3 percent), China (7.2 percent), and Italy (4.3 percent). By 2005 the World Bank had approved more than $8 billion in loans and International Development Agency credits. The U.S. government is the largest aid donor. Nigeria is a member of the World Trade Organization (WTO), the Organization of Petroleum Exporting Countries (OPEC), the Economic Community of West African States (ECOWAS), and, until spring 2006, served as chair of the African Union.

National and Military Politics

Nigeria returned to civilian rule in May 1999 after fifteen years of military rule. The 1999 constitution is based on a presidential rather than a parliamentary system. The president is elected for four-year terms, with a limit of two terms.[14] The first election was in February 1999, the second in April 2003, and the third in April 2007.

The legislative branch consists of a 107-seat Senate (with three from each of the thirty-six states, plus representation from the FCT at Abuja). The House of Representatives has 346 members, with distribution based on state and local populations. (The 2006 census came too late to affect redistribution of House seats.) Members in both the Senate and the House have four-year terms.

---

12. For background on U.S. perspectives on Nigerian oil, see David L. Goldwyn and J. Stephen Morrison, *Promoting Transparency in the African Oil Sector: Recommendations for U.S. Policy* (Washington, D.C.: Center for Strategic and International Studies, March 2004).

13. This privatization of oil refineries was one of the grievances in the national strike by the National Labour Congress (NLC) in June 2007.

14. Federal Republic of Nigeria, *Constitution of the Federal Republic of Nigeria, 1999* (Lagos: Federal Government Press, 1999).

The dominant political party is the People's Democratic Party (PDP), which in 2003 reportedly won about 62 percent of the presidential votes, although these figures were contested in the courts. (On July 1, 2005, the Supreme Court finally confirmed the national- and state-level figures.) In April 2007 the PDP was declared the winner in the presidential race with 72 percent of the vote, although most observers contest these figures (see chapter 4 for more detail). Based mainly in the north, the All Nigeria People's Party (ANPP) has been the major opposition party, which, along with about twenty-plus minor parties, has formed the Conference of Nigerian Political Parties (CNPP). In spring 2006, thirty-five political parties had been registered by the Independent National Election Commission (INEC), with additional parties emerging or realigning during the summer of 2006. By spring 2007, there were fifty registered parties, with about twenty-five contesting the presidency.

The importance of state and local politics cannot be overstated. Nigeria is a three-tier federation, with national, state, and local government responsibilities spelled out in the constitution. There are thirty-six states and 774 local government authorities, with legislative assemblies and councils respectively. Much of the funding for state and local government comes from block grant disbursements from the federal government based on national oil revenues. A complex constitutional provision designates how much each state receives from the federal distributive pool, depending on population, developmental level, crude-oil-producing capacity, and so on. In the 2003 elections the PDP captured twenty-eight governorships and the ANPP seven governorships (in the far north). The Alliance for Democracy (AD) captured the governorship of Lagos. In the 2007 election, the PDP claimed twenty-nine governorships, although at least fifteen of these have been contested in the election tribunal courts. Notably, the two major centers of opposition political parties are in Kano (All Nigeria People's Party) and Lagos (Action Congress), the two largest states in Nigeria.

Historically, much of Nigerian politics has revolved around the military. Nigeria became independent from Britain in 1960 and during the First Republic (1960–66) followed a Westminster parliamentary system. This system broke down in 1966 when junior officers attempted a coup and assassinated key northern regional and national leaders. The turmoil that followed led to the civil war (1967–70) in which the parts of the southeast zone (then known as Biafra) tried to break away. Between 1966 and 1979 a series of military regimes ruled. In 1979 there was a return to civilian rule under a Second Republic constitution, which was presidential in nature. In December 1983 the military again stepped in and established a series of regimes into early 1999, when the current Fourth Republic was inaugurated. (The so-called Third Republic was stillborn in 1993, when the elections of June 12 were annulled.)

Between December 1983 and May 1999, senior officers maintained consistently that they were trying to keep the country together, crack down on corruption, and serve as a transition to a workable system of democratic federalism. Critics of the military contend that they abused human rights, were equally corrupt, and delayed the development of democratic practices and civic cultures. Until 1999 many of the senior officers were from the north, although there has been a policy of recruiting officer candidates from each of the thirty-six states. Since 1999 and the transition to civilian rule, many of the former senior (northern) officers have retired, thus contributing to a sense of marginalization in the north.

The role of the police is also significant since all police are "federal," according to the 1999 constitution. How effective such police are in combating crime is very much a matter of political debate.[15] With more than 320,000 members, the police are by far the largest security agency in the country.

This brief profile of demographic, economic, and political characteristics provides the background for assessing Nigeria's influence and significance as a pivotal state within the larger African, Muslim, and global contexts. Clearly, there are serious sociopolitical challenges within Nigeria, and political leadership may well determine whether the country tips one way or the other on its pathway to the future. Issues regarding the ethnoreligious balance and the growing gap between rich and poor are at the heart of these challenges.

---

15. See Prince Charles Dickson, "The Nigeria Police: Going Nowhere Quickly," Jos, Plateau, Nigeria (www.gamji.com, accessed November 12, 2005), in which he decries the poor state of the police force, including its inability to combat crime despite attracting large numbers of recruits since 1999.

2

Sources of Nigerian Influence and Significance

An assessment of a pivotal state revolves around the nature of the influence and example of that state within its regional realm and also in a global context. Nigeria, through its political mechanisms and cross-cultural linkages, offers a primary model of a pivotal state attempting to achieve national unity by linking Muslim-Christian religious domains. The 2007 presidential election, in many ways, was a test of this model.

This chapter examines three major themes:

- what constitutes a pivotal state in the Muslim world, including types of potential pivotal Muslim states; the federal character model in Nigeria that attempts to create a level political playing field; Nigeria as a "people of the book" model and its role as a bridge between Muslim and non-Muslim cultural Africa; Nigeria's pivotal role globally as a major example of postcolonial development within an initially artificial set of boundaries;
- Muslim organizations in Nigeria and how they crosscut ethnoregionalisms, including the Sufi brotherhoods and the Izala movement; student and youth organizations; women's organizations; national umbrella organizations; antiestablishment organizations and networks;
- Nigerian links to transnational systems and issues, including nonstate and state-sector networks, international-security issues, and economic development.

The Idea of Pivotal States in the Muslim World

Most countries with large Muslim populations—Indonesia, Pakistan, Bangladesh, Egypt, Turkey, and Iran—are overwhelmingly Muslim in their demographics. (India is not included here because its Muslims are a clear minority.) By contrast, Nigeria has a large Muslim population but an almost equally large Christian element: about 50 percent Muslim and 50 percent Christian (and traditional religious believers). Middle-sized countries, such as Ethiopia or Sudan, are also faced with the challenge of creating a workable political system that bridges this religious identity divide. A westernized or Christianized southern zone and a Muslim interior zone characterize most of the smaller coastal countries in West Africa. Hence, Nigeria is clearly a prototypical test case in accommodating religious balance. Can a nation with about 70 million Muslims and about 70 million Christians set a pivotal or global example in terms of stability and progress?

In addition, because Nigeria is one of the major OPEC producers, it has an obvious significance in the global economy. As an example, in 1973 Nigeria helped break the Arab oil boycott of the West by increasing its production. Arab OPEC countries such as Algeria (32 million Muslims), Saudi Arabia (27 million Muslims), and Iraq (25 million Muslims) also are complex and obviously significant, but their internal dynamics revolve around factions and cleavages within the Muslim community (or *ummah*). Other major Arab countries such as Morocco—with 32 million Muslims—do not produce oil. The largest Arab state, Egypt—with about 73 million Muslims and 7 million Coptic Christians—is not in the major leagues of oil production. It does serve as a significant bridge figuratively and geographically along the Nile into sub-Saharan Africa and has always been part of African continental politics.

Nigeria, however, is very much part of the non-Arab state cluster within the global Muslim community, including Ethiopia, Tanzania, Mali, Senegal, Niger, Somalia, and Guinea in Africa and Turkey and Iran in the Middle East. The Central Asian cluster that includes Afghanistan, Uzbekistan, Azerbaijan, and Kazakhstan is becoming increasingly significant, along with Southeast Asia (such as Malaysia, Brunei, and Indonesia) and the giants of South Asia (Pakistan, India, and Bangladesh). As the Muslim world globalizes, it is increasingly clear that non-Arab cultures will play a significant role in its evolution and direction.

Relations between Muslim communities outside of the Middle East have become and will continue to be salient, and West African forms of Islam seem to be having an impact on Arab countries such as Morocco, Egypt, Sudan, and Saudi Arabia.[1] Historically, West African Islam has tended to follow the Sunni form of Islam and, within this tradition, Sufism.[2]

---

1. See, for example, "In Saudi Arabia, a Resurgence of Sufism: Mystical Sect of Islam Finds Its Voice in More Tolerant Post-9/11 Era," *Washington Post*, May 2, 2006. Thus, "The centuries-old *mawlid*, mainstay of the more spiritual and often mystic Sufi Islam, was until recently viewed as heretical and banned by Saudi Arabia's official religious establishment, the ultra-conservative Wahhabis. But a new atmosphere of increased religious tolerance has spurred a resurgence of Sufism and brought the once-underground Sufis and their rituals out into the open. . . . 'This is one of the blessings of September 11. It put the brakes on the (Wahhabi) practice of *takfir*, excommunicating everyone who didn't exactly follow their creed,' said Sayed Habib Adnan, a 33-year-old Sufi teacher. The government 'realized that maybe enforcing one religious belief over all others was not such a good idea.'"

2. See John N. Paden, *Religion and Political Culture in Kano* (Berkeley: University of California Press, 1973).

Three major political centers in Africa represent two great religious traditions: Egypt is predominantly Muslim, South Africa is predominantly Christian (and traditional), and Nigeria is religiously mixed (Muslim and Christian plus traditional). It is the challenge of bridging this religious divide that makes Nigeria a pivotal state.

The Federal Character Model in Nigeria

Several features of the Nigeria model are noteworthy in terms of politically bridging ethnoreligious and regional gaps. First, there has been a tradition of progressive conservatism that constitutes a strong political center and has always resisted more extreme forms of political belief. Second, religious and ethnic political parties have been banned (or denied recognition) in Nigeria since the colonial era. Third, national political parties require cross-regional alliances to be successful. Finally, the provisions for "federal character" in the constitution (and in accepted practice) have meant that each of the thirty-six states is entitled to representation in the executive (as well as legislative) branches of government. It is this power-sharing mechanism that has created a sense of a level playing field in the country's politics.

Thus, whether in the army, the police, the ministries, or the cabinet itself, every effort is made to include representatives from the diverse states. Originally, inclusiveness began as a northernization policy during the First Republic (1960–66) to include those from the Northern Region in government ministries.[3] This was to balance the overwhelming preponderance of those from the southern regions of Nigeria, who had more access to Western education and English language skills. In short, there was to be a rough parity between northern and southern Nigerians in the ministries.

In the aftermath of the civil war (1967–70) and the demise of formal regions, an informal attempt was made to achieve rough parity of state representation in executive appointments. With the creation of more states, especially after 1991, equal representation based on states became somewhat unwieldy, and the administration of General Sani Abacha (1993–98) proposed dividing the country into six geographical zones. The geographic designations, which were generally accepted by political elements, became surrogates for ethnoreligious or regional identities. The six zones are the northwest, north-central, northeast, southwest, southeast, and south-south.

The country underwent a series of military coups or leadership shifts between 1983 and 1998. With the return to civilian rule in 1999, the newly

---

3. See John N. Paden, *Ahmadu Bello, Sardauna of Sokoto: Values and Leadership in Nigeria* (London: Hodder and Stoughton, 1986). Ahmadu Bello, the first (and only) premier of Northern Nigeria (1960–66), was the architect of the "northernization" policy.

written constitution remained silent on the issue of north-south regional balance and of geocultural zones. It did, however, return to the idea of equal representation in the federal government of each of the thirty-six states. But in practice the idea of north-south balance is very much alive. It has always been the basis for selecting presidential and vice-presidential teams (even during the military periods).[4]

Likewise, the idea of representation by geocultural zones continues. For example, at the National Political Reform Conference in 2005, representatives were selected from each of the thirty-six states and then clustered within the six zones for purposes of caucusing and final reporting. In spring 2006, the failed attempt to authorize a third term for the president relied on zonal meetings to represent the thirty-six state assemblies. In 2008, the election reform commission is scheduled to hold public hearings in each of the six zones.

In this spirit of balance, the political question most paramount in Nigeria in 2005 and early 2006 was whether and how the presidential tickets for the 2007 election (which was the constitutionally mandated end of President Obasanjo's term) would be affected by the perceived need for regional rotation and balance. Thus, that Obasanjo was a Christian from the south and his vice president (Atiku Abubakar) a Muslim from the north suggested to many that the next ticket should be reversed, with a northern Muslim for president and a southern Christian for vice president.

A number of youth-oriented Muslim organizations in Nigeria (described below) seem keen to apply the federal character principle to religious-identity issues, as well as to the more obvious state, zone, or regional identities. They have counted the number of Muslims and Christians on various national councils and commissions and have argued for parity based on the federal character principle. Seeking to confirm their belief that Nigeria has a Muslim majority, they have also argued that the census in March 2006 should have included religious identity questions. Paradoxically, many Christian groups also argued for religious-identity questions in the census, convinced that Christians had become a majority.

Yet, the federal character model was not designed to accommodate religious identity, except in an indirect, proximate way. The basic assumption is that using state identities will cover the basic complexities of diversity in Nigeria, without some fine-tuning to address religious identity. Thus, citizens from Kano State are assumed to be Muslim, and citizens from Anambra State are assumed to be Christian. Some of the sharpest

---

4. See John N. Paden, *Muslim Civic Cultures and Conflict Resolution: The Challenge of Democratic Federalism in Nigeria* (Washington, D.C.: Brookings Institution Press, 2005). Also see Adeoye A. Akinsanya, "Federal Character in Nigeria: Bane or Blessing?" in *Nigeria in Global Politics*, ed. Alayiwola Abegunrin and Olusoyi Akomalafe, 31–46 (New York: Nova Science Publishers, 2006).

political contests occur, predictably, in the zones with an overlap of religious identities, such as the Middle Belt or the southwest.

The federal character model is also assumed (and constitutionally mandated) to apply at the state level. This means that each of the 774 local government authorities within Nigeria (and enshrined in the constitution) are entitled to representation at the state level. Clearly, those in state government are meant to show evenhandedness and not favor certain areas of the state over others. This takes on ethnoreligious significance in some of the Middle Belt states—such as Plateau State—where Christians are seen to be the dominant political power. It is also true in Kaduna State, where the northern portion, especially Zaria emirate, is predominantly Muslim and basically controls political power. The southern portion of Kaduna State is largely made up of smaller ethnic groups influenced by Christian missionaries.[5]

The priority of a workable political system in Nigeria (to be discussed in chapter 3) in part reflects the efforts to get the horizontal and vertical issues of federalism in balance. (Thus, the challenge is not just one of democracy in Nigeria but of democratic federalism.) Constitutional design features are also rooted in the evolving political culture consensus in Nigeria on issues of federal character. Yet, in the white heat of political campaigns and coalition building, some of these principles are likely to be breached. The basic challenge of democratic federalism in Nigeria is to produce leaders who have a long-term vision and will abide by guiding principles rather than temporary expediency.

Even political expediency, however, requires cross-regional (and hence cross-religious-identity) coalitions. No political party or candidate can succeed if he or she is unable to maintain a cross-regional coalition. While the military rulers, for the most part, have respected this principle, some of the civilian politicians appear to be less experienced in how to maintain local grassroots constituencies (that is, how to win state primaries) and then move to the center on matters of progressive conservatism and cross-regional alliances. This has been a major challenge of the 2007 elections at all levels.

Nigeria as a "People-of-the-Book" Model

Although the British joined Northern Nigeria and Southern Nigeria as a single entity in 1914, they administered the two regions de facto, as separate colonies. This changed after World War II when the decolonization process began. A fateful decision was made, both by the British and the

---

5. See Matthew Hassan Kukah, *Religion, Politics and Power in Northern Nigeria* (Ibadan: Spectrum Books, 1993). Also see Matthew Hassan Kukah, *Whistling in the Dark: Selected Interviews during the Abacha Era* (Sovereign Prints Nigeria, 2006).

Nigerians, to combine both regions into a political whole. (By contrast, the British territories of northern and southern Rhodesia became two separate countries: Zambia and Zimbabwe.)

During the pre–World War II period in northern Nigeria, the British, working through local, predominantly Muslim traditional authorities, had encouraged the idea of a "people of the book" (*ahl al-kitab*) formula for cooperation. Thus, Muslims and Christians felt they had more in common than they had with indigenous, animist (or polytheist) communities.

The first generation of northern leaders absorbed this model or paradigm. During the early independence era, there was close cooperation in the north between Muslims (whether emirs, civil servants, or teachers) and their Christian counterparts (whether chiefs, civil servants, or teachers). During this period, the premier of the Northern Region, Ahmadu Bello, initiated the northernization policy in which Muslim and Christian northerners were promoted rapidly, both at the regional and national levels. In the wake of the 1966 coup, key northern Muslim leaders were killed, including Bello, by junior officers mainly from the Christian southeast. Yet, after the countercoup in July 1996, it was a northern Christian officer, Yakubu Gowon, who was selected by the northerners to be the military leader for all Nigeria.

The people-of-the-book model continued in practice at the national level, through the federal character mechanisms and political coalition constraints mentioned above. There were stresses in this model, especially in 1986 when Ibrahim Badamasi Babangida announced Nigeria's membership in the OIC. In April 1990 disgruntled Christian army officers from the Middle Belt attempted to overthrow Babangida. Among other things, the officers declared they would excise the far northern (Muslim) states from Nigeria. The coup was put down, but interfaith tensions persisted.

The oil boom economy of the 1970s and 1980s brought opportunities for new business ventures in Nigeria. A common pattern was for military, political, and business partners to set up domestic joint ventures, which explicitly crossed religious and regional boundaries. Many of these political or business coalitions persist today and have thus linked the Nigerian power brokers into webs of interdependency.

In the late 1970s, decisions were made by the military to begin planning a shift of the capital from Lagos to Abuja. Subsequently, at the new federal capital in Abuja, every effort has been made to create the symbolism of tolerance and parity between Muslims and Christians. The national mosque in Abuja was planned with the idea that a national Christian cathedral would also be erected. Initially, divisions within the Christian communities disrupted plans for such a Christian edifice, but the interior of the Christian Ecumenical Center had been completed and the building dedicated by 2006. Exterior work, however, has continued into 2007. The center has been used for state occasions, such as the funeral for the wife of President Obasanjo and Remembrance Day.

Despite attempts at unifying efforts in the country's capital, including various national "peace committees," cooperation at the state and local levels has not always been easy. In particular, the fallout of sharia issues since 1999 in the twelve northern states has tended to harden Christian and Muslim identities. The challenges continue and are discussed further in chapter 4 (see map 3). The need for understanding among Muslims and Christians often permeates official visits by international delegations. In May 2006, for example, Vice President Atiku Abubakar welcomed to his office a six-man delegation of members from the Muslim World League, commending the league for "branches in Afikpo and Enugu. This will no doubt enhance the better understanding of Islam, having in mind that poverty and ignorance are definitely anti-Islam."[6] Afikpo and Enugu are in the southeast and predominantly Christian.

Koranic injunctions are used in public meetings to emphasize the theme of interfaith tolerance. At a national conference in Sokoto in December 2004 on the challenges of peaceful coexistence, Governor Alhaji Attahiru Bafarawa opened the proceedings saying "the Almighty created us in tribes and nations, so that we understand and relate well with each other and that best among us is he who fears God most, and he who fears God most is he who lives peacefully and harmoniously with his neighbor."[7]

Nigeria's Pivotal Role in Africa

Nigeria should not be considered a Muslim state in Africa, but rather a multireligious country with a secular constitution that serves as a bridge between Muslims and Christians in Africa. Because of its relative oil wealth and demographic resources, Nigeria is in many ways a key player in African affairs. Nigerian military peacekeepers have served in important roles worldwide, including in Liberia, Sierra Leone, Darfur (Sudan), and Democratic Republic of Congo.[8] And Nigeria holds a leadership position in West Africa through the Economic Community of West African States (ECOWAS) and in continental Africa through the African Union.

---

6. "Atiku on More Opportunities for Muslim Youth," *Daily Triumph*, May 12, 2006.

7. Ibrahim Jumare and others, eds., *Nigeria: The Challenges of Peaceful Co-Existence*, December 13–15, 2004. Conference proceedings (photocopied).

8. See Abiodun Alao, "Peacekeepers Abroad, Trouble-Makers at Home: The Nigerian Military and Regional Security in West Africa," in *Nigeria in Global Politics*, 63–78; Aderemi Ajibewa, "International Constraints on Foreign Policy Formulation: A Case Study of Nigeria and Regional Security in West Africa," in *Nigeria in Global Politics*, 79–94; Adebayo Oyebade, "Restoring Democracy in Sierra Leone: Nigeria's Hegemonic Foreign Policy in West Africa, 1993–1998," in *Nigeria in Global Politics*, 95–106.

Map 3   Nigerian States with Sharia Law, 2000

In addition to federal-level affairs, Nigerians in other domains are play-ing pivotal roles. Sometimes the line between state and nonstate initiatives gets blurred. The devastating locust infestation in the Sahel in 2004, which wiped out crops from Senegal to Chad, also affected the northern Sahelian states in Nigeria. States such as Sokoto also were hard hit but, because of their resource base, were able to provide seeds and fertilizers to farmers so that the 2005 agricultural season was not disrupted.

Yet, in neighboring Niger Republic, which borders at least five northern states in Nigeria (and shares several ethnic groups with northern Nigeria), the 2005 agricultural season was a disaster, resulting in famine and refugees. In July 2005 two of Nigeria's northern states—Jigawa and Yobe—offered direct assistance to populations in Niger Republic. Previously, Muhammadu Buhari, leader of the All Nigeria People's Party, had appealed to neighboring states and the Nigerian Red Cross Society to lead appeals funds for food and drugs for the peoples of Niger Republic. Buhari personally donated about N100,000 to Niger through the Nigerian Red Cross. According to newspaper accounts, "General Buhari said that watching news clips of the devastating effect of hunger and disease, especially on children, women and the aged people of the Republic of Niger should stir every African to action. 'This disaster has long been there, enough for any responsible government to arrest the situation—but alas, we have been caught unprepared again. . . . While I note the rather belated response of the federal government, effort ought to be made to sensitize private organizations and individuals to contribute more, not only in the spirit of African brotherhood but more importantly in the spirit of helping our neighbor.'"[9]

In short, Nigerian Muslims are fully aware of developments in the Sahelian zone, and, despite preoccupations with politics in Nigeria, are engaged in trying to alleviate the crises. Niger Republic is regarded by the United Nations as the poorest nation in the world. Its close proximity to Nigeria, and the arbitrary nature of the Nigerian border, has meant that events in Niger directly impact Nigeria. During an earlier drought in the Sahel, tens of thousands of refugees from Niger Republic crossed into northern Nigeria in 1979 and were absorbed through religious, kinship, and charitable connections.

The argument used in Nigeria for intervention in the crises in West Africa—both coastal and interior—has been "when your neighbor's house is on fire, your own house is not safe." In short, Nigeria has the will and the means to engage in crisis management in West Africa. It remains to be seen how effective Nigerians will be as peacekeepers in the Darfur crisis in Sudan, both through their key role in the African Union and through peace negotiation efforts in Abuja.

Nigeria's Pivotal Role Globally

Nigeria has significant links in Africa, in the developing world, in the Muslim world, and in the Western world. As of 2005 Nigeria stood as one of the major candidates for permanent membership on the UN Security Council. Nigeria's ambiguous status in the OIC may be a necessary condition for its larger role as a bridge between Muslim and Christian communities in Nigeria and worldwide.

On the Nigerian Christian side, one of the major candidates for the head of the Roman Catholic Church in April 2005 was Cardinal Francis Arinze of southeast Nigeria. He was identified, during the selection process, as someone who could reach out to the global Muslim community based on his experience in Nigeria. At the same time, many of the Muslim leaders in Nigeria have been active in interfaith dialogue not only in Nigeria but also within a global context. The emir of Kano (Ado Bayero) has been a preemi-

---

9. *Daily Trust*, July 28, 2005.

nent example of interfaith tolerance and cooperation at home and abroad. The new sultan of Sokoto, Sa'ad Abubakar, as formal leader of Nigeria's 70 million Muslims, has taken on this challenge as well.[10]

The Nigeria Inter-Religious Council (NIREC), consisting of twenty-five Muslim leaders and twenty-five Christian leaders, was revived in fall 2007 after several years of dormancy, in part under the influence of the new sultan, who serves as cochairman along with the president of the Christian Association of Nigeria. Rather than just meet in Abuja, beginning in 2008 NIREC is scheduled to hold quarterly meetings throughout each of the six geocultural zones. Sultan Sa'ad Abubakar also made a historic visit to the United States in November 2007. During this visit, he spoke at the United States Institute of Peace, where he discussed Muslim-Christian relations in Nigeria, called for strengthening the foundations of peace and religious harmony in Nigeria, and expressed the need to build bridges of understanding between Muslim and Christian communities.

Nigeria tends to alternate its ambassadors to the United States and the United Nations between Christian and Muslim representatives. This has created an impression that Nigerian diplomats are professional, knowledgeable, and cooperating members of the international community. The balancing of Muslim and Christian ambassadors is an extension, of sorts, of the federal character principle and is a symbol of interfaith balance. When Jibrin Aminu (a Muslim from Yola in the northeast) stepped down as ambassador to the United States in 2003, he was succeeded by George Obiozor (a Christian from the southeast).[11] When Obiozor stepped down in summer 2007, the chargé d'affaires a.i. was Ambassador Usman Baraya, originally from Argungu, Kebbi State. Nigeria opened a new embassy in Washington in 2002, and the structure is one of the most modern in the capital area, catering to the needs of Nigerians from every region and faith.

---

10. Sa'ad Abubakar was born August 24, 1956. He attended Barewa College, Zaria, before proceeding to the Nigerian Defense Academy, Kaduna, in 1975. He was commissioned in December 1977 as second lieutenant and posted to the Nigerian Army Armored Corps. He spent the next thirty-one years in the Nigerian Army, including in Sierra Leone (working with ECOWAS) and in Pakistan as Nigeria's defense adviser there, with concurrent accreditation to Iran, Iraq, Afghanistan, and Saudi Arabia, from February 2003 to February 2006. He returned to Nigeria after February 2006 to attend the senior-executive course at the National Institute for Policy and Strategic Studies, Kuru, where he wrote a research thesis titled "Religious Extremism as a National Security Problem: Strategies for Sustainable Solutions." He was appointed the twentieth sultan of Sokoto on November 2, 2006. As the new sultan, he is already playing a key role in interfaith cooperation and dialogue. "The Sultan of Sokoto, Alhaji Muhammad Sa'ad Abubakar III has expressed willingness and determination to work with the Christian Association of Nigeria (CAN) and other religious groups to end incessant religious crisis in the country." "Sultan: I'll Partner with CAN to End Religious Crisis," *ThisDay*, May 15, 2007.

11. Obiozor is originally from Imo state. Prior to his Washington assignment, he was Nigeria's ambassador to Israel. "Nigerian Envoy Seeks to Repair 'Uneasy Friendship' with U.S.," *Washington Diplomat*, August 2006, 15ff.

In short, Nigeria has enormous potential to play an important role globally and has made significant contributions to the cadre of international civil servants and diplomatic statesmen. For example, in 2007, Ambassador Ibrahim Gambari, originally from Ilorin, Kwara State, served as United Nations special envoy to Myanmar on behalf of UN secretary-general Ban Ki-moon. However, the country's internal stresses, unless addressed, may undermine the potential of Nigeria to continue its global role.

Muslim Identities and Organizations in Nigeria

Nigerian Muslim identities and organizations cover a full range of demographics and perspectives. Most are well within the mainstream of Nigerian society and thought. Following is a selected sample of such organizations to illustrate the nature of the spectrum. In general, the English names of organizations are used, except in a few cases where Hausa language is the commonly accepted basis of the acronym.

The key to understanding Islam in Nigeria is to recognize the central place of the Sokoto Caliphate, which serves as a framework or model even today. The Sokoto Caliphate, founded in the early nineteenth century by Usman Dan Fodio, continues to exert strong cultural influence in Nigeria and West Africa. Originally, the emphasis by Dan Fodio was on "justice"— including the removal of unfair taxes—and the need for Islamic education as a guide for the community. The challenge was to "polytheism" and "syncretism" prevalent in the Hausa states at that time. The founders of the Sokoto Caliphate, especially Usman Dan Fodio, his brother Abdullahi, and his son Muhammad Bello, were prolific writers in Arabic, Hausa, and Fulfulde. As of 2007, more than one hundred of their three hundred known works have been translated for publication in English and French.[12]

Five broad categories help to cluster contemporary Muslim identities and organizations within the broader historical and cultural context: Sufi brotherhoods and the Izala; student and youth organizations; women's organizations; national umbrella organizations; and antiestablishment networks, including the so-called Shiites and Taliban organizations. It is beyond the scope of this monograph to be systematic in recounting the origins, evolution, geographic distribution, and profiles of each group. Rather, the idea is to be illustrative and give a sense of central tendencies.

---

12. For more background on the Sokoto Caliphate, see H. Bobboyi and A. M. Yakubu, eds., *The Sokoto Caliphate: History and Legacies, 1804–2004*, vol. 1, *History, Economy and Society*, and vol. 2, *Values, Intellectual Tradition and Contemporary Significance* (Kaduna: Arewa House, Ahmadu Bello University, 2006). See also A. M. Yakubu, I. M. Jumare, A. G. Saeed, eds., *Northern Nigeria: A Century of Transformation, 1903–2003* (Kaduna: Arewa House, Ahmadu Bello University, 2005).

Sufi Brotherhoods and the Izala

The two main Sufi brotherhoods, Qadiriyya and Tijaniyya, both have a strong base in Kano in the north. The Izala movement sprang from a reaction against the Sufi brotherhoods after Nigerian independence by legalists who criticized Sufism as "innovation" and hence unacceptable. Although the Qadiriyya originally was associated with the Sokoto Caliphate, because of the perceived affiliation of the founders in the early nineteenth century, it came to be identified with Nasiru Kabara of Kano in the twentieth century. The location of his home and school, just opposite the central mosque and emir's palace in Kano City, gave the impression that the practice of Qadiriyya was part of the emirate establishment. That it was part of the "Fulani" ethnic side of the old city (as distinct from the "Hausa merchant" side of town) only strengthened that impression. Nasiru linked West African forms of Qadiriyya with a number of North African branches, such as the Shaziliyya (with its two subbranches, Arosiyya and Salamiyya), although over time the local Nigerian leaders tended to predominate over the original Arab leaders. Thus, Nasiru's main connections were with five main branches of Qadiriyya in Hausaland: Ahl al-Bayt, Kuntiyya, Shinqitiyya, Usmaniyya, and Sammaniyya.

Nasiru's trip to Baghdad (the international headquarters of Qadiriyya) in 1953 resulted in whole new sets of ritual practices in Hausaland, especially controlled breathing exercises and all-night drumming that could produce trancelike states. In 1958 Nasiru became head of Shahuci Judicial School and Library in Kano, and in 1961 he opened the Islamiyya Senior Primary School in Gwale ward. He served as a *tafsir mallam*, a teacher qualified to render the Koran into Hausa during the month of Ramadan. At the time of Nasiru's main influence in the 1960s, approximately 25 percent of Kano City residents were followers of this Sunni brotherhood. After Nasiru's death, his sons continued teaching at his school. At present, Kano still serves as the main Nigerian location for Qadiriyya teaching, practice, and group worship.[13]

Through much of the mid-twentieth century, Tijaniyya, also in Kano, was the dominant brotherhood in northern Nigeria. A traditional form of Tijaniyya stemmed from the nineteenth-century conversions by Umar Futi, a Tukulor Fulani from Senegal, and was based on individual, rather than group, supplementary prayers. With the arrival in Kano during World War II of Ibrahim Niass (a Wolof sheikh from Kaolack, Senegal), a "reformed" version of Tijaniyya developed and emphasized the use of group prayers. Initially it appealed to the Hausa side of Kano City, mainly traders and craftsworkers, and was led by the *mallams* from the Salga extended family,

---

13. See Paden, *Religion and Political Culture in Kano.*

commonly known as "Salgawa." Later, with the accession of Muhammad Sanusi to the emirship in 1954, Reformed Tijaniyya spread to all parts of the city and emirate, and indeed throughout the urban centers of Nigeria. The Tijaniyya was clearly the dominant Sufi brotherhood in Nigeria.

Reformed Tijaniyya also emphasized the need to modernize means of communication. This meant using radio and cassettes, photo-offset print media, and the Hausa language and led to a number of Reformed Tijaniyya youth groups. The Hausa long-distance traders, based in Kano, could stay in brotherhood guesthouses (*zawiyas*) throughout West Africa on their travels. Many chose to set up semipermanent residence in Kaolack, Senegal, to be closer to their spiritual leader, Ibrahim Niass. Although the international headquarters for Tijaniyya was in Fez, Morocco (at the tomb of Ahmed Tijani), it was less likely that northern Nigerians made that pilgrimage than Senegalese disciples, who were able to navigate through the French-speaking bureaucracy. In short, Kano became the major commercial center in Sahelian West Africa (and in northern Nigeria), and the Tijaniyya provided a link along the domestic and international trade routes.

With the death of Niass, his grandsons in Kaolack have continued the family tradition, and wealthy Kano merchants still send gifts and money to the Senegalese city. In Kano, with the death of former emir Sanusi, and spiritual leaders such as Tijani Usman, the Salgawa mallams on the Hausa side of the city have continued the Reformed Tijaniyya tradition, relying on wealthy Hausa merchants for support. The oil boom in Nigeria has produced a class of Hausa-speaking merchants who have the means to build mosques and schools and support brotherhood activities in Nigeria and throughout West Africa.[14]

By contrast, the Nigerian Izala movement, with its anti-Sufi bias, continues to be based in Kaduna—and to some extent Jos—which is inhabited more by civil servants and the site of modern light industry without the influence of the traditional Hausa merchants and traders. The key figure in this movement was Abubakar Gummi, teaching from his home in Kaduna. The full name for Izala is Jama'atul Izalatul Bid'ah Wa'ikhamatul Sunnah (Society against Innovation and in Favor of Sunna), and the organization is widely known by its Hausa acronym, JIBWIS.

Details of the competition between Kano and Kaduna, the two major cities in northern Nigeria, are beyond the scope of this monograph, but it came to a head in 1963 when the premier of the Northern Region, Ahmadu Bello, deposed Emir Sanusi of Kano on grounds of financial irregularities.[15] Since the death of Bello in 1966, there have been clashes between Izala youth

---

14. Ibid.
15. See Paden, *Religion and Political Culture in Kano,* and Paden, *Ahmadu Bello, Sardauna of Sokoto.*

groups, based in Kaduna and Zaria, and the youth wings of the Reformed Tijaniyya in Kano.

With the death in 1992 of the formative Izala leader, Abubakar Gummi, the Izala movement became decentralized.[16] The focus on "back to the Koran and Hadith," and the widespread availability of classical texts (including the Koran) in Hausa language, meant that a wide variety of interpretations became possible.[17]

It is important to emphasize that the Nigerian Izala movement is not co-terminous with Saudi Wahhabiyya or other forms of Salifiyya. While some elements of Izala may preach a more literal "back to fundamentals" (based on seventh-century precedents), other elements have been among the most modern elements in Nigeria. Certainly, Saudi influence has been significant in Nigeria, not least because oil wealth has allowed an increasing number of pilgrims each year. Yet, Nigerians and Saudis in the modern sectors have more in common as part of the global economy than as ideological soul mates. And Saudi officials are also aware of the strong Sufi legacy in West Africa and are keen to emphasize the Sunni connection rather than a Wahhabi connection. Finally, while the Izala movement appears consolidated, it is quite diverse and decentralized in practice.

Student and Youth Organizations

Five contemporary Nigerian student and youth organizations are described below to illustrate the variety of youth movements. On the student level, three are representative: the Muslim Students Society (MSS), the National Association of Muslim Law Students (NAMLAS), and the Muslim League for Accountability (MULAC). Of the youth organizations, the most important is the National Council of Muslim Youth Organizations of Nigeria. Smaller groups are also salient in light of contemporary politics, for example, the Global Network for Islamic Justice, based in Zamfara State.

The MSS of Nigeria was founded in 1954 in Lagos and in 1956 was based at the University of Ibadan. The predominantly Yoruba students opened a branch at Ahmadu Bello University (Zaria) and Abdullahi Bayero College (Kano) in 1963. In 1969 the national convention elected a Hausa student from Kano as president. By 1970 there were four hundred branches throughout Nigeria located at secondary schools and universities, and a faculty-level organization was set up to parallel the student organization. Weekly meetings were held to discuss Islamic issues, and students were encouraged to help teach Arabic and religious knowledge in primary schools. All

---

16. See Abubakar Gumi (sic) (with Ismaila Tsiga), *Where I Stand* (Ibadan: Spectrum Books, 1992).

17. For background on Izala, see Ousmane Kane, *Muslim Modernity in Postcolonial Nigeria: A Study of the Society for the Removal of Innovation and Reinstatement of Tradition* (Leiden and Boston: Brill, 2003).

communications within MSS are in English, including the national journal, *Muezzin*. Patrons include most of the major Muslim political-religious leaders in Nigeria. Throughout its history, the theme of MSS has been to emphasize Muslim unity in Nigeria. At present, it is very much part of the establishment in Nigerian higher education and has been influential in the "peace committees" on many higher-education campuses.

More specialized Muslim student organizations have emerged, especially during the Fourth Republic. Of particular significance, given the sharia law issue, have been the NAMLAS and the MULAC, both emerging on northern campuses. MULAC was set up as a male counterpart to the Federation of Muslim Women's Associations of Nigeria (FOMWAN), in which cohorts of women students had helped monitor the 1999, 2003, and 2007 elections. In addition to helping monitor elections, MULAC sought to promote good government. NAMLAS, MULAC, and FOMWAN are very much part of the establishment.

In terms of general youth movements, the largest organization is probably the National Council of Muslim Youth Organizations (NACOMYO) in Nigeria. As with the MSS, it began as a predominantly Yoruba federation of organizations and is still dominated by groups from the southwest, which often take a critical stance on government policies. The national secretariat is located in Ikeja, Lagos. In general, NACOMYO has insisted at every turn that Muslims be represented in the political life of Nigeria. In 2005 this took the form of protesting the lack of Muslim representation (especially from the southwest) at the National Political Reform Conference. Protesters noted that of the 382 members in the conference, only 165 were Muslims compared to 217 Christians. NACOMYO has also been critical of the relative lack of Muslims on the 2005–06 national census council, arguing that "the outrageous and obnoxious appointment of 15 directors of the 2006 population census with 12 Christians and 3 Muslims makes one lose confidence in the headcount from the start."[18]

Finally, a youth group called the Global Network for Islamic Justice (GNIJ) appears to have emerged in the wake of civilian rule in 1999 and is based in Zamfara State. As noted, the sharia issue began in Zamfara, and this organization seems to be a strong proponent of strict sharia law. Members have been active in Internet communications on a wide range of related issues in Nigeria since 1999.[19]

---

18. See http://AmanaOnline.com/articles/art1129.

19. See, for example, from the group's Web site, *"Almajirance*: The Menace of Child-Begging: Control and Solution" and "Being a Proposal Submitted to Zamfara State Government with Special Consideration to Shari'ah Practicing in Northern States of Nigeria," P.O. Box 55, Gusau, Zamfara State, glonij@justice.com (December 2003).

Women's Organizations

The Muslim Sisters Organization (MSO) was set up at universities in Kano and Zaria in the early 1980s to offset the influence of the so-called feminist organizations such as Women in Nigeria (WIN). The MSO has continued on campuses but has become a part of FOMWAN, the dominant women's organization in Nigeria.

FOMWAN's constitution came into effect in October 1985. The headquarters rotates, depending on where the president (*amirah*) is living. (The presidency rotates between states on an annual basis.) FOMWAN was set up to counteract the role of "custom," that is, traditional ethnic culture, in Nigerian Muslim society. In the early 1990s, it had four hundred member associations, of which about three hundred were in Yorubaland. By 2003 there were more than five hundred associations nationally, with most in Yorubaland. The national secretariat is in Abuja. English is the official language of FOMWAN. As noted above, FOMWAN has become an active civic organization on a wide variety of fronts.

Other Muslim women's civic organizations include Professional Muslim Sisters Association (PMSA), based in Abuja, which renders "professional and financial assistance to the less privileged members of society, particularly women and children."[20] PMSA has helped to establish women's health and legal aid clinics schools for disadvantaged children, orphanages, and rehabilitation centers for the disabled and for drug addicts, and has begun a microcredit scheme for women.

Other civic groups include the Women's Rights Advancement and Protection Alternative (WRAPA), founded in 1999, which has provided legal assistance to women in many of the sharia court cases. In general, WRAPA has been critical of the way sharia law in the northern states has impacted women. A Muslim women's organization, BAOBAB, has been especially active in contesting sharia laws that affect women unfairly.[21] BAOBAB is effective in part because it has attracted educated northern Muslim women who understand local cultures.

National Umbrella Organizations

One of the earliest umbrella organizations—embracing a wide range of participants and perspectives—was the Jama'atu Nasril Islam (JNI, or Society for the Victory of Islam), set up in January 1961 in Kaduna by Premier Ahmadu Bello. Its focus was northern Nigeria, and it assumed

---

20. Professional Muslim Sisters Association, pamphlet.
21. See Mohammed T. Ladan, *A Handbook on Sharia Implementation in Northern Nigeria: Women and Children's Rights Focus* (Kaduna: League of Democratic Women [LEADS-Nigeria], 2005), especially chapter 3, "Comments on Safiya Hussaini and Amina Lawal's Cases Decided by Sharia Courts," and chapter 4, "Annotated Decisions of Nigerian Courts Relevant to Women and Children's Rights," http://www.leadsnigeria.org.

that every Muslim in the region was a member of the JNI. Abubakar Gummi was a key member of the Central Caretaker Committee, and most of the other members were senior civil servants. In 1964 its influence was extended during the inaugural meeting under the chairmanship of *waziri* Junaidu of Sokoto. The sultan attended, as did representatives from each of the northern provinces. The JNI built a headquarters and an Islamiyya school in Kaduna. After the death of Bello in 1966 and the dissolution of the Northern Region in 1967, the JNI ceased to receive government support but continued to be led by Abubakar Gummi. It focused increasingly on Muslim unity within Nigeria and internationally.

Yet the JNI has remained primarily a northern organization. It has stressed modern education and, in 1967, established the Sheikh Sabbah College in Kaduna with help from the Kuwaiti Sabbah family. The college was the first Muslim secondary school in northern Nigeria. In 1972 it was taken over by the North-Central State government as part of a policy to control all parochial schools. Subsequently, the JNI has continued to be active as a non-governmental organization within Nigeria but with a special sphere of influence in Kaduna State and parts of the north. Sultan Sa'ad Abubakar has attempted to revive the JNI in 2007. However, its role has been assumed partly by the Nigerian Supreme Council for Islamic Affairs (NSCIA), which has a more clearly national focus, and is presided over by its president-general, Sultan Sa'ad Abubakar.

In 1974 Muslim leaders from throughout Nigeria met to consider creation of a new organization to cater to the needs of Muslims throughout Nigeria and to serve as a channel of contact with the government on matters of interest. The NSCIA was officially inaugurated in 1974. In the 1980s it became more active under the leadership of Ibrahim Dasuki and Abdul-Lateef Adegbite. After Dasuki became sultan of Sokoto in 1988, he assumed the post of president-general of NSCIA. The deputy president-general was Mustapha Umar El-Kanemi, shehu of Borno, and the secretary-general was Abdul-Lateef Adegbite, seriki of Egbaland. Vice presidents were drawn from the (then) thirty states of the federation. The design of the organization is "federal" but with the three top leaders drawn from the Sokoto caliphate, Borno, and Yorubaland—the three major Muslim culture zones.

The constitution of the NSCIA identifies scope and structure as follows: promoting Islamic solidarity among Muslims in Nigeria and other parts of the world and coordinating external contacts with the Nigerian government and with foreign governments on Islamic matters. The eleven main standing committees are elders, official opinions (*fatwa*), finance, conversion campaigns (*da'wah*), research and policy, youth and social welfare, media, international relations, economic affairs, legal affairs, and pilgrimage.

With the deposition of Ibrahim Dasuki by Sani Abacha in 1996, the leadership of NSCIA went to the incoming sultan of Sokoto, Muhammadu

Maccido.[22] Until his death in October 2006, Sultan Maccido continued to play an active role in NSCIA, encouraging cooperation throughout Nigeria. As noted, his successor, Sa'ad Abubakar, was selected on November 2, 2006, and formally installed on March 3, 2007. Regular NSCIA meetings are often held at Arewa House in Kaduna, the former home of Northern Region premier Ahmadu Bello and now a research center affiliated with Ahmadu Bello University. Arewa House also serves as a conference center with a focus on peacebuilding and conflict resolution in northern Nigeria.[23]

The NSCIA is obviously an establishment organization with both traditional and modern components. It is often seen as the counterpart to the CAN, which is the umbrella organization for the very diverse spectrum of Christian groups, ranging from Roman Catholic and mainstream Protestant to the Yoruba "praying people" movement (Aladura) and inspirational, evangelical, and Pentecostal churches.

With the return to civilian rule in 1999 and the establishment of sharia law in the criminal domain in the twelve northern states, new Muslim organizations have emerged in support of this development. A national umbrella organization, of sorts, has been the Supreme Council for Sharia in Nigeria (SCSN). The SCSN tries to coordinate sharia law across the twelve sharia states, and encourages the extension of sharia in the civil domain in southwestern states. The relationship of the NSCIA and SCSN is not quite clear, but the latter has a special focus on legal domains.[24]

In addition, regional umbrella groups have emerged during the Fourth Republic, notably, a forum of Northern States Traditional Rulers[25] and a Southwest Muslim ummah conference.[26]

---

22. See Abdulkadir Adamu and Muhammadu M. Gwadabe, *Alhaji Muhammadu Maccido Abu-bakar III, The 19th Sultan of Sokoto: The Bridge Builder* (Zaria: Amana Publishers, 2005).

23. See H. Bobboyi and A. M. Yakubu, eds., *Peace-Building and Conflict Resolution in Northern Nigeria: Proceedings of the Northern Peace Conference* (Kaduna: Arewa House, Ahmadu Bello University, 2005).

24. See "Conference of Muslim Organizations Supreme Council for Shari'ah in Nigeria," glonij@justice.com, August 24, 2005, AmanaOnline (accessed September 5, 2005). Thus, "The leaders and representatives of some Muslim Organization under the auspices of the Supreme Council for Shari'ah in Nigeria (SCSN) met on Saturday, 15th Rajab, 1426 (20th August, 2005) to discuss important national issues. At the end of their deliberations, the Conference of Muslim Organization (CMO) took the following decisions:" The topics on which positions were taken included: "i. Child rights law; ii. Attempt to cover up the case of American terrorist caught with explosives and arms in Plateau State; iii. Marginalization of Muslims in Nigeria polity; iv. National census; v. Famine in Niger Republic and the abject poverty of millions of Nigerians." The conference called on state governments to release grains from their strategic reserves to bring down the cost of grains.

25. See "Constitutional Amendment Divides Northern Emirs," *ThisDay*, April 30, 2006.

26. See "South-West Muslims Now under One Umbrella," *Daily Triumph*, May 3, 2006. Thus, "Worried by the lack of cohesive leadership and unity among their members, Muslims in the South West yesterday resolved to come together as a body to speak with one voice. This is one of the highlights of a five-point resolution reached at the end of a one-day Stakehold-ers Summit of the South West Muslim Ummah held in Ibadan, Oyo State. The group, under the interim leadership of Prof. Babatunde Fafunwa, resolved to speak with one voice on

Antiestablishment Networks

A Muslim youth group emerged in the north during the military period (1984–99). Called "Shiites" by the Nigerian Muslim establishment, members of the group referred to each other as brothers (*ikhwan* or *'yan brotha*). Economic problems at the time, few prospects for some graduates of Ahmadu Bello University (ABU) in Zaria, and the prohibition on political forms of protest all contributed to this youth group's formation.

Inspired by the Iranian Revolution, and apparently with funding from Iran, Ibrahim Zakzaky, an economics graduate from ABU, challenged the corruption of the Nigerian military regimes and called for a return to an Islamic model of government. Zakzaky and his followers clashed with authorities in Katsina in 1991. Finally, in 1996, Zakzaky was jailed by the Abacha regime. With the Fourth Republic, he was released and has continued to be an active critic of the Muslim establishment in Nigeria. For example, in June 2005 there were confrontations between "Shiite" groups and the emirate authorities in Sokoto over access to the central mosque.

Despite efforts by the northern establishment to co-opt the "Shiite brothers," they have resisted, for the most part, from being included in the formal umbrella organizations described above. Although they did not engage in ostensible violent behavior immediately after the return to civilian rule,[27] this changed on July 18, 2007, when a Sunni cleric, Umar Dan Maishiyya, was killed while leaving a mosque in Sokoto. He had been leading the verbal attacks on the Shiites in Sokoto, calling them "infidels." His death sparked reprisals and the killing of at least five Shiites and the destruction of scores of homes.

An even more violent network has emerged since 2003, sometimes called "the Taliban." In December 2003 an incident occurred in Yobe State in the

---

matters of development and welfare of the Muslim community in particular and humanity in general. . . . The group, which is yet to adopt a name, noted that its guiding principle shall at all times be consulting themselves in offering comments and solutions on matters of Islamic and national interest. . . . Earlier in his welcome address, Prof. Fafunwa had explained that the group decided to focus on the South West because Muslims in the region had suffered double disadvantage as the south is generally regarded as 'Christian' in spite of the preponderance of Muslims." Abdul-Lateef Adegbite, secretary-general of the Nigerian Supreme Council of Islamic Affairs (NSCIA), the Aare Musulumi of Yorubaland, Alhaji Abdul Azeez Arisekola Alao, and representatives from Ekiti, Ogun, Ondo, Oyo, Osun, Lagos and Oyo states also attended the conference.

27. During the Abacha military period in the 1990s, the Shiites became a presence in Kano, often attracting young men who could not afford to pay the bride price for marriage but who were attracted to the traditional Shiite doctrine of "temporary marriages" practiced in the Middle East. Their dress became distinctive, and they celebrated such Shiite festivals as Ashura during the month of Muharram. Increasingly, the Shiite identity became self-ascriptive. Yet, according to scholarly studies of this movement, the basic theology is still Sunni. See Kane, *Muslim Modernity in Postcolonial Nigeria*.

northeast. According to the UN Office for the Coordination of Humanitarian Affairs,

> A student-led Islamic sect launched an armed uprising . . . with the aim of setting up a Taliban-style Muslim state in northern Nigeria. . . . [T]he authorities were swift to quell the insurrection. However, political analysts and security officials fear the emergence of the Al Sunna Wal Jamma (Followers of the Prophet) may be an indication that extremist Islamic groups have found enough foothold in Nigeria to make Africa's most populous country a theatre for worse sectarian violence than it has seen in recent years and actions of terrorism.[28]

The fact that the leader of the group had taken the name "Mullah Umar" and that the group was flying the flag of the Taliban in Afghanistan raised questions as to whether a Taliban organization had indeed emerged in Nigeria.

Although most members of the Yobe "Taliban" group were killed by the police, the remnants appear to have dispersed throughout northern Nigeria. While the number in this group is estimated by Nigerian authorities to be small (perhaps in the two hundred to three hundred range), they are well organized and structured. They are armed and actively recruit. Their main focus seems to be on the Nigerian government, which is seen as a puppet of the United States and Great Britain. Their goal is to establish an Islamic government throughout Nigeria. The extent of external support and funding the group receives is not clear. The network, or structure of the organization, is very much underground, but it appears to be drawing on educated (or semieducated) young people who are disillusioned with what they perceive as the injustice of the current situation in Nigeria. Nigerian religious leaders who have met with members of this group suggest there is a lot of idealism but not much serious religious knowledge informing the group. Indeed, the term "taliban" has been used for centuries in northern Nigeria in reference to students of Islam and does not have the negative connotations common in the West.

Adding to the ambiguity of the "Taliban" phenomenon is an incident in Kano that occurred between the April 14 gubernatorial election and the presidential election on April 21, 2007. Rumors were rampant. Kano sources and the media characterized the so-called Taliban as a community of about 200–300 people, including men with red headbands and women who were completely covered in Afghan-style burqas, who, along with their children, had come from outside Nigeria—from Niger or Chad—and not speaking

---

28. Integrated Regional Information Network/IRIN, "Nigeria: Muslim Fundamentalist Uprising Raises Fear of Terrorism," January 25, 2004.

Arabic or Hausa. Since they did not speak Hausa or Arabic, the assumption was that they must have come from the east—Chad or Borno—rather than the north. This community was located near the waterworks in Challawa just outside of Kano City. Apparently, it had been there for some time, trading with local Kano people, via hand signs, their needs for food and water. A clash with local authorities in mid-April 2007 led to the killing of more than a dozen police. After burying their own dead, the "Taliban" group simply disappeared. Subsequently there has been almost no mention of this group in the press, even though some were caught unexpectedly on the road to Kaduna in a roadblock after the presidential election.[29] Some observers describe the group as a cultlike "flight" (*hijra*) group, although such a distinctive group would have been noticed by local village heads or district heads. Given the tensions of the election and the attempt of the PDP federal government to unseat the stronghold of the All Nigerian People's Party (ANPP) in Kano, many speculated locally that the government may have been behind this "timely" event. Others see it as related to the killing of Sheikh Ja'afaru Adam (noted earlier). Some local observers describe the Kano "Taliban" as "hired bandits from Chad." Kano State set up a commission of inquiry, but no report has been issued as of fall 2007.

In November 2007, Nigerian authorities arrested five so-called al-Qaeda militants in the north, accusing them of preparing to attack government facilities, and reported that three of them had received training in a "terrorist camp" in Algeria. Many informed Nigerians dismiss this claim. Clearly, disillusioned youth in the Muslim north are an issue of concern to the Nigerian government, to the established Muslim organizations, and to the international community.[30] Given porous borders, the possibilities for

---

29. A large truck was stopped at a routine checkpoint on the Kaduna road and was found, surprisingly, to be filled with so-called "Taliban." This suggests some sort of logistical infrastructure to the group, since they had access to weapons and transportation. At the time of the presidential election, there were many rumors as to the identity of the group, from Shiites (because of their dress) to remnants of the Maitatsine movement, to north African al-Qaeda affiliates, to Chadians, among others. The bottom line was that most observers agreed that they were not Nigerians, although even this is open to question. The "Taliban incident" caused the cancellation of a trip to Kano by international observer groups to oversee the election. The author was privileged to discuss this issue with the deputy inspector general (DIG) of police in Abuja, April 19, 2007, although at the time the police were very uncertain as to what was happening. The DIG indicated that the police were flying a plane over the Kano area to try to identify the area where the "Taliban" were located.

30. By coincidence, in late April, the U.S. State Department issued its controversial report stating that Nigeria was becoming a "terrorist camp." This added to the perception in opposition areas of northern Nigeria that the Obasanjo government was working to create a sense of crisis, which could even justify state of emergency decrees. See "U.S. Report Names Nigeria as 'Terrorist Camp,'" *Guardian*, May 2, 2007. Thus, "A report by the United States (U.S.) government has listed Nigeria as a recruiting group for terrorist organizations. The report added that not only are there individuals with suspected ties to terrorist groups around the world in Nigeria, such activities as recruitment of terrorists are common trends in the country. . . . According to its yearly report titled 'Country Reports on Terrorism,' the U.S. said, 'While the Nigerian government did not support international terrorism or terrorists,

transnational network links are high. How the dynamics play out in this establishment versus antiestablishment confrontation, which so far has been quite localized, remains to be seen. Clearly, an overreaction by the authorities in their hunt for "terrorists" would exacerbate the situation.

Nigerian Links to Transnational Systems

Much attention is given to Nigeria's leadership role in the fifteen-member Economic Community of West African States (ECOWAS) and the fifty-three-member African Union (AU). Many ECOWAS facilities are in Abuja (including secretariat offices and a parliamentary convention center). Nigeria has provided the bulk of the military resources used to stabilize countries in West Africa, such as Liberia and Sierra Leone, through the organization's military component known as ECOMOG.[31]

The African Union (AU), launched in 2002, evolved under the chairmanship of Nigerian president Obasanjo until new leadership emerged in spring 2006. Successor to the Organization of African Unity (OAU), the AU includes the Peace and Security Council, the Continental Early Warning System, the African Standby Force, and the Council of the Wise. The AU is heavily involved in Sudan through its African Mission in Sudan (AMIS), which began in June 2004 as an observer mission and within a year had evolved into a military force with 2,300 troops deployed in the Darfur region. Most of these troops were Nigerian. In 2007, there was an agreement that a hybrid AU/UN peacekeeping force of considerable size would be established in Sudan, although this remained under negotiation with the government in Khartoum. Nigeria has been much more reluctant to contribute to an AU peacekeeping force in Somalia, which is seen as beyond its national sphere of concern.

The porous and fragile nature of international boundaries in Africa have contributed to a natural linkage between Nigeria and its neighbors. When the boundaries were drawn by Europeans at the Berlin Conference (1884–85), often straight lines on a map, as a prelude to "the scramble for Africa" by Britain, France, Germany, and others, Nigeria's major ethnic groups were separated by country borders. Nigeria shares the Hausa-Fulani, a major group, with Niger Republic, the Yoruba, a dominant element, with Benin Republic, the Igbo with southern Cameroon; and the Fulani with northern Cameroon.

---

there were some individuals and private groups in the country with ties to probable terrorist elements in Sudan, Iran, Pakistan, and Libya. Members of terrorist groups, including al-Qaeda and the al-Qaeda in the Islamic Maghreb and Salafist Group for Preaching and Combat (AQIM/GSPC) have operated and recruited in Nigeria.'"

31. See Abegunrin and Akomolafe, eds., *Nigeria in Global Politics*.

The intense debates in the early postcolonial era wrestled with the question of whether the artificial colonial boundaries should be respected, or whether there should be an attempt to reconstruct some semblance of precolonial logic to the political communities. It was agreed in 1963, with the founding of the OAU, to respect the inherited colonial boundaries as a way to avoid irredentism, bloodshed, and perpetual conflict. But the underlying realities persist and have become more apparent as trade links between English- and French-speaking countries in West Africa have deepened, perhaps mirroring the closer ties between Great Britain and France within the European Union.

Nonstate Transnational Links

At the same time, in the interior of West Africa and in many of the coastal cities, Hausa has become the major lingua franca for grassroots level commerce, much as Swahili has been in East Africa. The oil-backed Nigerian currency (naira) is used widely throughout West Africa. Many of the newer Nigerian industries are producing goods distributed throughout the region.

Since much of the focus in this monograph is on the predominantly Muslim areas of northern Nigeria, the geographic regions of the country should also be explored. The ecology of West Africa (and Nigeria) is divided essentially into two zones: savanna and rain forest. Much of the savanna region—between the Sahara desert to the north and the rainforest to the south, from Senegal in the west to Chad in the east—is overwhelmingly Muslim. Many basic trade and migration patterns in the savanna zone thus move from west to east. This is also the historic pilgrimage route to Mecca and Medina, which continues from West Africa through Chad and Sudan to the Arabian peninsula. One of the major ethnolinguistic groups in West Africa, the Fulani (also called Peul and Fellata) spread from Senegal to Sudan. The Fulani were also the major factor in establishing the Sokoto caliphate in the nineteenth century, which stretched from Niger through Nigeria and into Cameroon. Many of the early Sufi leaders were Fulani. Because of the pastoral herder nature of Fulani groups, as distinct from the settled agriculture of the Hausa, they were often identified by their clan names even though linguistically they were considered Fulani.

After the Muslim reformist movement conquered the Hausa states in the early nineteenth century, the high degree of intermarriage resulted in what is now designated as a Hausa-Fulani group (with Hausa as the lingua franca rather than Fulfulde). Rural Fulani, sometimes called Bororo, still speak Fulfulde and move their cattle around in northern Nigeria, depending on the seasons. The bloody conflict in 2004 in Plateau State was largely between herder Fulani and local settled agricultural groups, whom the Fulani accused of stealing their cattle and not respecting the traditional rights of usage to graze in return for manure on their fields. The farmers, in turn, accused the Fulani of ruining their crops by moving cattle through the fields. The fact that the Fulani were Muslim and the local farmers were largely indigenous religious followers or Christian added to the perception that this was a religious conflict.

The historic links between northern Nigeria and Sudan are important to understand in light of contemporary politics. Nearly one-quarter of the Muslim population of contemporary Sudan is regarded as "Nigerian"—often a term meaning "West African," because of historical migration patterns, especially by Fulani (Fellata) groups. The situation is complicated by the fact that Nigerians consider themselves African, while many Sudanese see their identities as Arab, African, or Arab-African. Notably, African identities in Sudan may include Christian ethnic groups in southern Sudan and also Muslim ethnic groups in the west. Often "African" is used to indicate "non-Arabic-speaking" populations. (Arab is not a racial category, because Arabs may be of any physical type, but rather it represents a language category, that is, those who speak Arabic as their first language. Thus, in Nigeria, the Shuwa Arabs in the northeast are indistinguishable physically from other Nigerians.) This is a delicate issue since Arabic-speaking Sudanese also regard themselves as African, and Sudan has always been a member of the OAU and, more recently, the AU.

This issue is most clear in the conflict in the western region of Darfur ("The Land of Fur") between Muslim settled African farmers (especially the Fur groups) and Muslim Arabic-speaking herder-raiders, known as *janjaweed*, who are in alliance with the powers in Khartoum. There is great variety among the non-Arab groups in Darfur, as there is among the Arab clans, and it would be a great mistake to see the Darfurian crisis as simply African versus Arab.

Khartoum has long been not only an epicenter of Arab culture and influence but also a confluence of sub-Saharan and north African populations. During the colonial era, many northern Nigerians were sent by the British to Khartoum (or its neighboring twin city, Omdurman) for higher education, especially in Arabic and Islamic legal studies, which were essential in administering sharia law. Khartoum was considered "safer" by the British than places such as Cairo. As a result, many of the first generation of legal scholars in northern Nigeria after 1960 were trained in Khartoum, including the grand *khadi* of northern Nigeria, Abubakar Gummi. Because Khartoum was also on the pilgrimage route from Nigeria, some of the early Nigerian diplomats were sent to Khartoum as "pilgrimage officers," including Ibrahim Dasuki (who later became sultan of Sokoto, 1988–96).

In the 1960s and 1970s, many of the senior professors at Ahmadu Bello University in Zaria and Bayero University, Kano especially in the fields of law, Islamic studies, and Arabic, were seconded from universities in Sudan. They were English speaking and professional and made a real contribution to the establishment of higher education in northern Nigeria. Some even self-identified as Fulani. Over time, they were replaced by a new generation of northern Nigerian scholars, some of whom had studied in Khartoum or Omdurman.

An equally important feature of northern Nigerian links in West Africa has to do with the Senegalese connection, through the Tijaniyya Sufi brotherhood. North Africa was off-limits to West Africans during World War II because of the fighting, and, as a consequence, Kano became a major military base and airport during World War II. Cut off from northern routes, Muslim Sufi leaders in Senegal began to make the pilgrimage by way of Kano. In particular, Sheikh Ibrahim Niass of Kaolack, Senegal, became linked to the emirate authorities in Kano and also to some of the long-distance Hausa trading groups. While many in Kano were already affiliated with the Tijaniyya through the nineteenth-century efforts of Umar Futi, the spread of Reformed Tijaniyya, linked to Niass, became a major pattern in the post–World War II era and into the early independence period. From Kano, the movement spread throughout northern Nigeria (except Borno) and well into the southwest.

The emir of Kano, Muhammad Sanusi, was the key connection with Ibrahim Niass. A successor to Sanusi, Ado Bayero, who came to the emirship in 1963 and was still serving as of 2007, had previously served as Nigerian ambassador to Senegal, in part because of the large number of Kano (and Nigerian) pilgrims who were making visits to or settling in Kaolack. Many of the Kano long-distance traders, that is, those functioning throughout Nigeria and West Africa, were affiliated with the Reformed Tijaniyya brotherhood. Thus, a strong transnational link was established with areas that had previously been off limits to Nigerians, the French-speaking areas of West Africa. And, as previously noted, the Hausa language, rather than English or French, has become the lingua franca of the grassroots commercial world.

Ibrahim Niass was also a key liaison with the international base of Tijaniyya in Fez, Morocco, and he had excellent ties with the Saudi royal family. On many occasions he accompanied senior Nigerian pilgrims on pilgrimage to Mecca and Medina. That he was a West African Sufi was less important to the Saudis than his Sunni credentials and their obvious desire to establish ties with Muslims in West Africa. Niass's Nigerian base in Kano, rather than Sokoto, also was important given the growing tensions between Sokoto and Kano in the early independence era. Yet, the influence of transnational Sufism in the postindependence era was now a permanent feature of the Nigerian scene. The other major Sufi brotherhood in northern Nigeria, the Qadiriyya, under the leadership of Sheikh Nasiru Kabara of Kano, also became involved in transnational links, especially with Sufi groups in North Africa. The international base of Qadiriyya was at the Baghdad tomb of the founding saint, Abdul Qadir al-Jailani, but there is little evidence that West Africans visited Baghdad as a pilgrimage site. The dominant feature of both Tijaniyya and Qadiriyya in Nigeria was their insistence that local West African rather than North African Arabs assume leadership roles.

The stage was now set for the ideological confrontation between those northern Nigerians who followed Sufism (of whatever variety) and those who were of a younger generation. The latter tended to be Western educated and felt they did not have time for the voluntary Sufi prayers and rituals but wanted to get back to the Koran and the sunna—that is, the actions and sayings of the Prophet Muhammad—as their sole reference in religious practice. The oil revenues of the 1970s and thereafter made possible a rapid expansion of secondary schools and university facilities. As noted, English was the medium of instruction, which facilitated the access of a whole generation of northerners to the broader English-speaking world, including portions of the Muslim world.

Abubakar Gummi was the principal leader and teacher of this Koran and sunna movement, which became known, as discussed earlier, as the Izala. From his home base in Kaduna, Gummi led a life of piety and teaching, especially after the dissolution of the northern Nigeria region in 1966. Prior to 1966, he served as grand khadi, or chief Islamic law officer and judge, in northern Nigeria. An outstanding Arabic and Islamic scholar, Gummi also interpreted the Koran into Hausa, which made it more widely available to non-Arabic-speaking local constituencies.[32] Trained in Khartoum, Gummi was the main liaison to the Saudis for senior Nigerian pilgrims and could garner international support (mainly from Gulf and Saudi Arabian sources) for schools and mosques in Nigeria.

In short, Nigerian Muslims have a strong legacy of transnational links, whether of the ethnic variety—the Fulani throughout West Africa and the Hausa in Niger—or of the religious variety—Senegal, Morocco, Sudan, and Saudi Arabia. Historically, the trans-Saharan trade routes to Algeria and Morocco were also significant, and some ethnic groups, such as the Tuareg, who live mainly in what is now Mali and Niger Republic, as well as Nigeria, were skilled in facilitating such trade. Commercial cities such as Kano were the sub-Saharan entrepôts, receiving and sending goods to North Africa.

More recently, with the widespread use of English after about 1970, northern Muslims had access to Muslims in Great Britain and throughout the British Commonwealth countries. At the same time, Hausa language also became a lingua franca in northern Nigeria and in many parts of West

---

32. See *Alkur'ani Maigirma Zuwa Harshen Hausa* [The Glorious Koran in Hausa Language], interpreted by Abubakar Gummi, n.d.

Africa. Many of the upcoming generation of northern university graduates were thus fluent in English, Arabic, and Hausa (plus, in some cases, a variety of indigenous mother tongues). This multilingual capacity is quite remarkable. As the post–cold war era of globalization unfolded (including new technologies of communication and transportation), northern Nigerian Muslims were feeling confident in their place in the larger political and economic scheme of things.

Yet, with the death of Gummi in September 1992, new patterns of Islamic practice emerged as the Izala movements (based as they were on the Koran) moved to a wide variety of local interpretations and leadership patterns. By 2000, with sharia law in the twelve far-northern states, there was no single formula or pattern. Some of the local patterns of ethnoreligious conflict throughout the north also had very different root causes. Additionally, the diffusion of authority and the ready access to Koranic sources meant that those younger Muslims educated in the languages and ideas of transnational contexts had a variety of lifestyle, political, and religious options, including flight (*hijra*) from the "land of injustice," that is, Nigeria in its oil boom "get-rich-quick" mode. The gap between grassroots, or civil society, and the infrastructure and transnational reach of the Nigerian state grew wider, especially during the military period between 1984 and 1999.

State-Sector Transnational Links

In many ways, the state-based subregionalisms of Africa have been the building blocks for the AU. ECOWAS has been the key structure in West Africa. Other African subregional components include the East African Community (EAC), the Intergovernmental Authority on Development (IGAD), the Common Market for Eastern and Southern Africa (COMESA), and the South African Development Community (SADC). Headquartered in Addis Ababa, the AU, as mentioned, has an African Mission in Sudan (AMIS) and one in Burundi (AMIB).

The formation of the AU emerged between 1999 and 2002. The Sirte Extraordinary Session in 1999 designed the AU, and the Lome Summit in 2000 agreed to the Constitutive Act of the Union. The Lusaka Summit in 2001 designed the implementation process, and the Durban Summit in 2002 launched the AU and witnessed the First Assembly of Heads of State of the African Union. While all AU members are equal, clearly Nigeria, Libya, and South Africa (plus to a lesser extent, Kenya and Algeria) dominate and often pay the dues for the less-rich states. The involvement of the AU (especially Nigeria) in Darfur to protect civilians emphasizes the reality that Nigeria is becoming the colossus of Africa—a point not always appreciated by smaller, non-energy-producing states. Since prior to 2007 the United Nations Security Council had been unable (or unwilling) to get involved in Darfur, Nigeria had become crucial in convening peace talks in Abuja and in supplying peacekeeping groups. The 2006 Abuja accords were intended as a peace settlement but fell apart because some rebel groups were not represented. As noted, in 2007, the United Nations Security Council has been edging toward supplementing the AU involvement in Darfur, pending negotiations with Khartoum. In October 2007, peace talks were held in Sirte, Libya. Yet, several of the Darfurian "rebel" groups were reluctant to go to Libya, in part because it was an Arab state. Meanwhile, twenty-six thousand UN/AU peacekeeping troops were scheduled to go to Sudan in early 2008.

The AU has also been directly involved in discussions regarding reform of the UN Security Council. In July 2005 the fifty-three members of the AU proposed that six new permanent members be added to the Security Council, two of which would be from Africa. Presumably Nigeria and South Africa would be the leading candidates, although Egypt was also contesting for the position. President Obasanjo had suggested publicly on numerous occasions that since one in five black people in the world is Nigerian, it would be appropriate for Nigeria to be a permanent member. With the expectation in 2005 that the 2007 Nigerian presidential elections would produce a northern and Muslim president, this would mean that, for the first time, a Muslim-led country would be a permanent member of the UN Security Council.

The politics of the United Nations have shifted since 2005, but the election of Umaru Yar'Adua in 2007 does provide a Nigerian Muslim civilian president for the first time since 1983. The UN Security Council membership issue was still under discussion within the General Assembly in 2007, but back room negotiations have not reached any consensus on enlargement of the council or on which African country would be the choice for the seat.

Also, as of 2005, former president Obasanjo may have been more popular in the international community than he was at home. But the attempt to change the constitution to allow for a third term and the obvious rigging of the 2007 election has altered many of these perceptions. On May 16, 2006, the Nigerian National Assembly rejected efforts to change the constitution to allow for a third term, but Obasanjo's international reputation was already damaged. President Yar'Adua's participation in the UN General Assembly session in September 2007 was well received and served as his major debut on the international scene. His modesty, integrity, and intelligence are appreciated, but he still remains an unknown quantity in the eyes of many at the global level.

At the same time, Nigeria has been very active in a range of other international organizations, including OPEC, where Rilwan Lukman from Kaduna has played a key role as secretary-general. Lukman has served a record eight times as president and secretary-general of OPEC and is highly regarded as a leading international statesman. He served as a minister in the first administration of President Obasanjo (1999–2003), but he became disillusioned with the money politics and heavy handed role of the president and returned to the OPEC headquarters in Vienna.

In the World Trade Organization (WTO), Nigeria has been a strong proponent of eliminating agricultural subsidies in the advanced industrial countries. President Obasanjo was a guest observer at the G-8 meeting in Scotland in July 2005 and, given the London bombings that occurred during the conference, was seen to be a strong ally in the global war on terrorism. The next year the G-8 apparently declined to invite Obasanjo because of his efforts to extend his administration beyond its two-term constitutional mandate. The June 2007 G-8 summit in Heiligendamn, Germany, included President Yar'Adua, despite domestic protests in Nigeria over the flawed election. Two of the key issues at the G-8 in Germany were Africa and climate change.

Nigeria's involvement with the Commonwealth Heads of Government Meetings (CHOGM) has been rocky, but the country now plays an active role in it. During the Abacha period, the British Commonwealth expelled Nigeria after the 1995 hangings of dissidents (including Ken Sara Wiwa) who had been implicated in the murders of some traditional rulers in the Delta area. But in December 2003, the meetings convened in Abuja and were attended by Queen Elizabeth II.

Most salient from the perspective of this monograph, Nigeria joined the Saudi-inspired OIC in 1986 under the Babangida administration. In part, this was as a political balancing act by Babangida who was in the process of recognizing Israel. Nigeria had ruptured relations with Israel in 1973 after the OAU expressed concern that "Israeli forces crossed the West Bank into Egypt, hence African soil."[33] Egypt was a member of the OAU, and African states protested the Israeli invasion as an act of solidarity.

The guidelines for OIC membership at that time were that a country should be at least 50 percent Muslim and have a Muslim head of state. When Nigeria was accepted by the OIC, a political crisis developed in the country, with the CAN protesting. Subsequently, Nigeria has been represented at OIC summits by diplomats or senior officials and has tried to downplay the controversy. At the same time, the OIC remains an official observer at the United Nations and is very much a part of the international community.

The 2004 OIC summit in Malaysia, at which the three-year leadership term shifted from Qatar to Malaysia, represented a wide cross section of Muslim countries and societies and saw observers from Russia, India, and other nations. With a Muslim president of Nigeria in 2007, it is not clear

---

33. See Alufolajimi Adejokun, "Nigeria and Israel: Change and Continuity in Diplomatic Relations," in *Nigeria in Global Politics*, 172.

whether Nigeria will be more active in the OIC. (In general, Nigerian voters focus more on domestic issues than international ones.) Yet, the pattern is clear. Since the inception of the Fourth Republic—and especially since the 2003 surge in oil prices—Nigeria is playing an increasingly pivotal role in international affairs.

Issues of International Security

The new global realities since September 11, 2001, include the fact that non-state networks have attacked not only Western interests abroad (embassies in Africa, naval ships, and other targets) and Western countries at home (London and Madrid) but also Muslim civilians in places as diverse as Morocco, Indonesia, Turkey, and Saudi Arabia. The al-Qaeda network and its affiliates are presumed to be active in at least sixty countries. Osama bin Laden has specifically mentioned Nigeria as ripe for Islamic revolution. Not surprisingly, the Nigerian government takes this threat seriously, as do others in the international community.

Official Nigerian government statements claim that there are no al-Qaeda cells in Nigeria, and most U.S. officials agree.[34] Nigerian immigration authorities have turned back certain Pakistani preachers at the Lagos airport. Nigerian police and military were involved in violent clashes with so-called Taliban elements in Yobe in December 2003, in which dozens were killed. The Nigerian State Security Service (SSS) and National Intelligence Agency have been very active within Nigeria. In early spring 2007, the SSS detained suspects in Maiduguri for questioning in Abuja. And the Kano incident in April 2007 has been mentioned above.

Yet the prevailing mood within the northern Muslim community seemed to be skeptical, sensing that the Obasanjo government was using this issue to increase its powers, appease its foreign allies, and intimidate its political opposition. Since many in southern Nigeria (and in the international community) have only stereotypes in mind when it comes to the Nigerian Muslim community, the whole question of perceptions and definitions becomes critical. Many southern Nigerian publications tend toward an alarmist position, complete with doctored photos, claiming that the "jihadists" and "terrorists" from the north are somehow trying to take over Nigeria. The ethnoreligious clashes in Plateau State and Kano in May 2004 added fuel to this perceptual fire. The earlier clashes in Kaduna, including the so-called Miss World riots in late 2002, were seen as part of vast Islamist conspiracy. The symbol of "sharia" was used to mobilize Christian

---

34. See Princeton Lyman and J. Stephen Morrison, "The Terrorist Threat in Africa," *Foreign Affairs* (January-February 2004), 75ff. Yet, note Nigerian government allegations in November 2007 that five "al-Qaeda" members intended to attack government facilities in three of Nigeria's largest cities.

groups. Terms like "Wahhabi" and "Izala" appeared in some elements of the Nigerian press and Internet as synonymous with terrorists.

As Nigerian politics prepared for the 2007 elections, these perceptual challenges and negative attacks on individuals and groups increased, especially against the major leader of the opposition, Muhammadu Buhari. The need for communication, education, and mediation could not have been greater. Into this mix, the real security concerns of the international community became extremely sensitive. A storm of protest and resentment broke out in the Nigerian press and on the Internet when, in spring 2005, parts of a U.S. National Intelligence Council (NIC) report from January 2005 were published, suggesting that Nigeria might become a failed state. The U.S. naval presence in the Gulf of Guinea also became an issue in the Nigerian press, including questions as to how much transparency the Nigerian government was providing. An editorial in the Lagos- and Abuja-based *ThisDay*,[35] a news daily generally sympathetic to the government, expressed concern that the Nigerian government was not sharing with the Nigerian people the country's emerging military links with the United States in the volatile Gulf of Guinea coastal waters.

Clearly, U.S.-Nigerian naval cooperation in a globally significant oil zone has taken on more importance since 9/11. While turmoil in the on shore and off shore oil-producing areas of the Delta has been essentially a Nigerian domestic matter since the early 1990s, it now caught the world's attention. International oil companies often are required to provide their own security,[36] and the kidnapping of expatriate oil workers, which has happened at both onshore sites and offshore rigs, inevitably is a matter of international concern, especially for the countries whose citizens are involved.

---

35. "US Navy in Gulf of Guinea," *ThisDay*, July 5, 2005. Thus, "with the news of increased presence of US naval ships in the Gulf, Nigerians are still largely in the lurch as to what it all represents. The little that is known about the military manoeuvre came from the US military authorities. It took weeks before the Nigerian Army volunteered a terse statement. A spokesman of the US military said that deployment of troops in the Gulf region which began six months ago, is to 'deter potential terrorists in the global war on terrorism as well as counter its proliferation and organized crime.' Admitting increased deployment of US marines in the Gulf, US authorities said the troops are there not only for training exercise but to enhance quick response to possible terrorist attacks within the West African region whose strategic importance to the US has been on the rise. US's increasing dependence on oil from the Gulf of Guinea nations makes it easy to understand any military involvement by the country in the region. The country's annual West African Training Course (WATC) which started since 1979 is perhaps one evidence of its increasing concern about the security situation of the region."

36. "Shell to Acquire 70 Boats to Boost Security in N/Delta," *BusinessDay* (Lagos and Abuja), May 17, 2006. Thus, "Royal Dutch Shell, the Anglo-Dutch energy group, has issued a tender for about 70 boats in an effort to strengthen security in Nigeria's delta region. According to a Shell tender document obtained by the Financial Times and dated January of this year, the boats would be required '24 hours a day, seven days a week . . . to support round-the-clock drilling and production operations of Shell.' Shell has been the target of attacks in the Niger Delta this year. The attacks have cut oil production by 455,000 barrels per day, basically halving output, and coincided with the kidnappings of several Shell oil contractors."

Since the coastal oil-producing areas of Nigeria are outside the Muslim demographic zone, the tensions are more often between elements of local ethnic communities, such as Ogoni, Ijaw, and Itsekiri. Confrontations have also occurred between local groups, often unemployed youth, and the Nigerian government, or the international oil companies, or both. The Nigerian military has been used, sometimes in a heavy-handed manner, to put down local unrest. Hence, the increasing cooperation of U.S. and Nigerian military units raises larger issues, not only of sovereignty but also of how ordinary people perceive the global war on terrorism. The need for conflict resolution is critical as an alternative to military action.

The increasing emphasis on far offshore, deep-water drilling, plus the political insistence that the international oil companies do more refining in Nigeria, joins the issue of domestic and international security concerns. While turmoil in the oil-producing areas of Nigeria has not been linked to al-Qaeda types of activities, the Nigerian government is increasingly likely to take preventive, rather than reactive, approaches to security issues in these areas. In all likelihood, this means closer cooperation with elements of the international community. The need for appropriate political leadership on all sides is imperative to manage the sensitivities of these issues and to provide effective deterrents to international criminal activities.

Transnational Issues of Economic Development

The contemporary global economy has largely bypassed Nigeria, except in the oil-producing industries. In part, this has been a legacy of political disengagement during the military regimes of the 1990s, although the environment has changed dramatically since 1999. But global economic actors also are watching Nigeria for signs of corruption and bureaucratic mismanagement.

For example, although a U.S. consortium produced the master plan for the federal capital in Abuja in the late 1970s,[37] very few U.S. companies were involved in the design and construction efforts. Japanese and German companies, who were not under the constraints of the U.S. Foreign Corrupt Practices Act, took the lead. Subsequently, U.S. pressure led countries within the Organization for Economic Co-operation and Development (OECD) to take a tougher line on corruption, including not allowing "facilitation fees" as tax-deductible business expenses.

Despite congressional restrictions on aid to OPEC countries, the Nigerian transition from military to civilian government in 1999 allowed Congress

---

37. See *The Master Plan for Abuja: The New Federal Capital of Nigeria* (Federal Capital Development Authority, 1979). The author was one of two U.S. social scientists who participated in this project.

to fund a series of "transition initiatives," administered by USAID, to strengthen this democratic development. The international community has had a real stake in the success of democracy in Nigeria. During her term, Secretary of State Madeleine Albright selected Nigeria as one of four countries to receive special resources in its transition to democracy. Subsequently, the war on terrorism has resulted in concessionary aid in a variety of ways.

Yet, as noted, economic development is primarily a domestic matter. The unusual advantage that Nigeria has is not only its oil wealth but also its human capital. These human resources are dispersed internationally. How they interact with domestic interests and resources remains to be seen. The international community is well aware that Nigerian criminal groups have become globalized—especially in the area of drugs and confidence scams. Yet, there have been increasing instances where overseas Nigerians are using their resources in a legitimate and constructive way in their home areas and within the Nigerian macroeconomic environment.

In short, Nigeria may be at a tipping point, toward either constructive development or a situation in which turmoil and corruption prevail. The efforts of the former finance minister, who has World Bank experience, and her "dream team" of economists may have been a necessary but not sufficient condition in effecting meaningful reforms. The real direction will be set by broad segments of Nigerian society as they come to grips with the challenges of nation building.

Finally, because of its "mono-crop" economy (that is, its oil and gas), Nigeria has had less contact with Arab business communities, except through OPEC. The Lebanese merchants in Nigeria—mainly Maronite and Shiite—have gradually been displaced by the emerging Nigerian business class. As Nigerian oil wealth circulates at higher socioeconomic levels within society, some of the Nigerian Muslim oil beneficiaries are exploring investment opportunities in Dubai and the Gulf states.

In overview, the sources of Nigerian influence and significance within the Muslim world revolve around its demographic size, its oil economy, its prototypical West African approach to religion (including Sufism), its people-of-the-book balance of identities, and its experiments with political mechanisms (such as the federal character approach) to accommodate ethnoreligious diversity. Historically, Islam in Nigeria has had trans-Saharan connections with North Africa, but, more important, it has provided the west-east links in the Sahelian zone of West Africa. In the postindependence era, and with oil revenues coming on stream, the Nigerian links with Saudi Arabia have increased through pilgrimage opportunities and through an increased awareness of their joint Sunni heritage.

3

Challenges of Nation Building

The primary task of any nation is to get its domestic house in order. A country's abilities to act within the international domain are highly dependent on its internal conditions. Nation building and economic development require vigilance and constant confrontation with challenges. In order of priority, the five challenges that Nigeria now faces are as follows: establishing a workable political system, consolidating rule of law, developing capacities for conflict resolution, facilitating economic development, and stemming corruption at all levels. Unless these challenges are met, it is hard to imagine Nigeria playing a constructive international role. Indeed, the erosion of these capacities may portend a failure of the state system in various domains. State failure would turn Nigeria from a positive example of a pivotal state to a negative one.

Establishing a Workable Political System

The Fourth Republic constitution promulgated in May 1999 in the final days of the military administration is similar to the 1979 constitution, that is, an American-style presidential system with a bicameral legislature and an independent judiciary. However, as noted, Nigeria is a three-tier federation, with national, state, and local responsibilities delineated in the 160-page constitution. (A major difference from the U.S. constitution is that all police in Nigeria are federal.) Military and selected civilian leaders drafted the document in 1998–99, ensuring the main focus was on a speedy transition to civilian rule. Indeed, the election of civilian officials at all three levels occurred in late 1998 and early 1999, prior to the unveiling of the constitution in May. This hasty election left many in Nigeria feeling a need for further discussion and possible amendments to the constitution after 1999.

This constitutional debate, of sorts, occurred during the second Obasanjo administration. In spring 2005 the president established a National Political Reform Conference (NPRC) in Abuja to discuss possible changes in the national political formula. The conference consisted of nearly four hundred delegates, nominated by the president and the state governors, who were instructed that, apart from the two "no-go areas" of national unity and federalism, all issues were on the table. The categories of delegates are shown in table 2.

TABLE 2   DELEGATES TO NATIONAL POLITICAL REFORM
              CONFERENCE, 2005

Category	Number of Delegates
"Elders"	45
Retired military personnel	3
Retired police personnel	2
Retired State Security Service (SSS)	2
Retired civil servants	2
Retired diplomats	2
Traditional rulers	8
Universities	6
Nigerian Employers Consultative Association	6
Nigerian Youth Organizations	6
Women's groups	6
Manufacturers Association of Nigeria (MAN)	6
Nigerian Association of Chambers of Commerce, Industry, Mines and Agriculture	6
People's Democratic Party	12
All Nigeria People's Party	4
Alliance for Democracy	0
Other parties	2
Civil societies	6
Muslim leaders[a]	6
Christian leaders	6
Nigerian Union of Journalists	1
Newspaper Proprietors Association of Nigeria	2
Nigerian Labor Congress	6
Trade Union Congress (TUC)	2
National Association of Nigerian Students	2
Nigerian Guild of Editors	1
Physically challenged people	3
Nigerians in Diaspora	5
Sociocultural groups:	
Arewa Consultative Forum	4
Afenifere	1
Ohanaeze	2
Middle Belt Forum	2
Ijaw National Congress	3
Special cases	5
Subtotal	175
State representatives[b]	218
Total	393

a. Muslim leaders included the following: Umaru Aliyu Shinkafi, (Zamfara)
    (later replaced by Bashir Sambo after Shinkafi was injured in an accident);
    Ibrahim Tahir (Bauchi); Ishaq Oloyede (Ogun); Abdulkadir Orire (Kwara);
    Adam Idoko (Enugu); and O. R. T. Okiri (Rivers).

b. Six from each of the thirty-six states, plus two from Federal Capital Territory.

At the 2005 conference, the key issue for delegates turned out to be the formula for the "distributable pool" of oil revenues going to the thirty-six states. In particular, the portion of oil revenues to go to the oil-producing states was highly contentious. A deadlock emerged between the south-south and the northern-zone delegates. South-south delegates walked out on June 14 over a recommendation that the percentage going to oil states be increased from 13 percent to only 17 percent. They demanded 25 percent, graduated to 50 percent over the next five years. To break the impasse, a committee representing state delegations and one member from each of the six geopolitical zones met in July 2005 to consider the resource-control question and other difficult issues, such as local government funding, federating units, rotational presidency, banning of ex–heads of state, and service tenure for the president. The committee also addressed controversies such as the method of selection of local government chairmen, state creation issues, legal immunity for office holders, the idea of state police, and the role of the Independent National Electoral Commission (INEC) in relation to local government elections.

Recommendations and submissions from a wide variety of sources from throughout the federation were submitted to the NPRC. One trial balloon was to establish a one-term presidency of six years, making it possible for then-president Obasanjo to extend his second term by two years beyond 2007. The Kano emirate council also submitted some fundamental recommendations on a wide range of issues, including consultations, consensus building, and constitutional, political party, electoral, judicial and legal, civil society, police and prison, and government-structure reform. Basically, the Kano emirate council favored a return to the First Republic model, including a role for police at the local level. Debate at the conference over many of the issues was very open and covered extensively in the media. Controversy was endemic, as several of the smaller political parties boycotted the proceedings, claiming the People's Democratic Party (PDP) had stacked the conference with its stalwarts.

The political impact of these deliberations remains uncertain. The open discussion process is healthy in a democratic system, but any real impact on constitutional revisions may be limited. According to the constitution, the amendment process resides with the National Assembly and not with any appointed body. In late July 2005, the NPRC report (with majority and minority views) was submitted to the National Assembly. Yet, during that summer, the National Assembly was at loggerheads with the president, and most members—including those in the PDP—were skeptical about giving up any more powers to the executive branch. With the 2007 elections looming, the real competition for power had already begun.

The central issue until mid-May 2006 was whether the constitution should be amended to allow the president to compete for an additional third term (and in some versions, with the same provisions for the governors). By then, about 116 constitutional amendments were under consideration by the National Assembly, including the third-term amendment. Yet, the political backlash against a third term resulted in the Senate turning down all proposed changes on May 16, and the issue became moot.[1] On May 18 President Obasanjo accepted the results of the Senate deliberations.[2] Immediately after the Senate decision, the political season opened up among factions and personalities, in prelude to the party nominating conventions scheduled for fall 2006.

Meanwhile, on July 1, 2005, the Nigerian Supreme Court rendered its judgment on the 2003 election contest, confirming the 2003 presidential election results. The political focus then shifted to Muhammadu Buhari of the ANPP and other opposition parties for a reaction to the unfavorable decision. Without free and fair elections, despair sets in, and Buhari's press conference on July 1, 2005, as reported on the Internet, went to the heart of the matter:

> This morning the Supreme Court of Nigeria upheld the decision of the Court of Appeal that the 2003 Presidential Election result be allowed to stand. The decision flies in the face of facts, of law and of common sense. It is a political—not a legal judgment—and Nigerians will regard it as such. . . . ANPP and myself as their Presidential Candidate went to Court to protest the way and manner in which the Independent Electoral Commission (INEC) conducted the 19th April, 2003 Presidential Election. We appealed to the Supreme Court complaining about the Court of Appeal's dismissal of our petition despite its finds of proof, and existence of undisputed evidence of substantial non-compliance with several fundamental provisions of the Electoral Act 2002. These include widespread violence of alarming magnitude which had resulted in numerous brutal killings of members of the ANPP, their supporters and in-

---

1. The Nigerian press was dominated by coverage of the "third-term" debate. See, for example, "3rd Term: Governors Give 3 Conditions to Obasanjo," *ThisDay*, April 21, 2006; "Protesters Stone Obasanjo's Convoy in Kano: President, I've No Hands in Tenure Elongation," *ThisDay*, April 25, 2006; and "Pandemonium as Senate Refuses to Include 3rd Term for Governors," *ThisDay*, April 26, 2006.

2. See "National Assembly's Action Is Victory for Democracy, Says Obasanjo," text of Obasanjo's speech at an emergency meeting of the National Executive Committee (NEC) of the People's Democratic Party (PDP), www.Gamji.com, May 18, 2006, 5. Thus, Obasanjo says: "The National Assembly as the constitutional and legitimate body for making laws for this country including the supreme law of the land—the constitution—has just concluded as it deemed fit, especially the Senate, the exercise on the amendment to the Constitution of the Federal Republic of Nigeria. The outcome is a victory for democracy. There is no absolute right and absolute truth except God. And in any argument or debate, there is bound to be an element of right and wrong or truth and untruth on either side. And we must respect each other no matter the human verdict and human foibles."

nocent passers-by in several states of the country. The conduct
of the elections was accompanied by unprecedented magnitude
of brazen electoral malpractices by INEC in its official capacity,
undue influence by the President through his illegal deployment
or armed soldiers and police accompanied by party thugs during
the purported elections. . . . Although now thoroughly disappointed by the decision, yet, consequent upon our belief in, and
commitment to, the enthronement and sustenance of true democracy based on the rule of law, and the imperative of respecting the final pronouncement of the body charged with nurtur-
ing the supremacy of the rule of law, on our part we accept this
decision of the Supreme Court, although we do not agree with it.
But all the virtues of democracy we subscribe to will not lead to
the existence of a stable society, unless people submit to certain
rules of conduct. Where the government and its agencies do not
subscribe to any rules and the Judiciary places them above the
rule of law and the constitution, it only leads to the triumph of
despair over hope.

Clearly, the essence of a democratic political system is transparency and
accountability. In the Nigerian case, a robust opposition party or parties
committed to constitutional rules would enhance this. The acceptance of
the Supreme Court decision by the ANPP is a milestone in the journey
toward a workable political system. Yet, even the PDP-dominated National
Assembly continued with its efforts to impeach President Obasanjo in summer 2005, on grounds of arrogating powers to himself that were not in the
constitution.

Major issues remained in the effort to move from personality politics—
especially the role of Obasanjo—to system-capability enhancement.
The elections of 2007 continued to draw intense interest, especially on
the presumed shift of presidential power from the south to the north.[3]
There were strong ethnoreligious implications to this potential shift,
although Nigeria has devised a variety of surrogate mechanisms to blur
these underlying realities. At base, coalitions are needed to link across
north-south regions and the six geocultural zones. Can Nigeria develop
a political system that can accommodate the extreme ethnoreligious and

---

3. Throughout the period of third-term debate (late 2005–spring 2006), northern political
   leaders insisted on a power shift to the north. See "2007: Northern Govs Insist on Power
   Shift to North," *ThisDay*, November 25, 2006. Thus, "Worried by the growing campaign for
   a third term in office for President Olusegun Obasanjo, the Northern Governors' Forum
   (NGF) rose from its meeting in Kaduna with the assurance that they remained committed
   to power shift to the North in 2007."

regional diversity of the country and also strengthen principles of justice and law widely accepted by civil society?[4]

Throughout the second half of 2006 a broad spectrum of officially recognized political parties emerged, although few had selected presidential candidates.[5] The party names and acronyms, as shown in box 1, clearly reflect party themes and aspirations, such as "democracy," "progressive," "action," "redemption," "justice," and "united." More salient, the focus on "alliance," "peoples," "Nigerian," and "African" suggests a clear sense that Nigerians are ready to transcend religion and ethnicity in terms of their political party futures. The number of registered parties also suggests that the next stage would have been coalition building across parties. After the initial publication of the INEC list in March 2006, several additional parties were registered, bringing the total to about fifty. Key governors, such as Alhaji Bafarawa (Sokoto), set up the Democratic People's Party (DPP), which served as a platform for his presidential bid. The vice president, Alhaji Atiku Abubakar, set up the Action Congress (AC) when he broke with the PDP and, despite PDP legal objections, the AC constituted a major challenge to the incumbent party. Yet, only in the final days of the 2007 presidential campaign were there serious efforts at opposition-party coalition alliances, and even these proved unworkable. In short, the large number of opposition parties—no doubt encouraged by the PDP—split the vote against the incumbent party.

In the aftermath of the 2007 election, there was an effort to balance the zones of the country in terms of key appointments. Since President Yar'Adua was from the northwest and Vice President Jonathan was from the south-south, the office of senate president was zoned to north central, while that of the Speaker of the House of Representatives went to the southwest. The southeast was allocated the office of deputy senate president and the office of head of the civil service of the federation. The Northeast zone got the office of deputy speaker as well as the secretary to the government of the federation (SGF). Every state is represented on the Federal Executive Council (FEC).

---

4. See, Attahiru M. Jega, *Democracy, Good Governance and Development in Nigeria* (Ibadan: Spectrum Books, 2007). For an earlier discussion of these issues, see Attahiru Jega, ed., *Identity Transformation and Identity Politics Under Structural Adjustment in Nigeria* (Kano: Centre for Research and Documentation, 2000).

5. Independent National Electoral Commission, *List of Registered Political Parties with Their Acronym and Logo* (Petra Digital Press, March 2006). Also, see Independent National Electoral Commission, *Political Party Finance Manual* (Abuja, March 2005). Subsequently, other parties were also recognized, including Accord, Action Congress (AC), Democratic People's Party (DPP), National Majority Democratic Party (NMDP), National Democratic Solidarity Party (NDSP), National Unity Party (NUP), Nigeria Elements Progressive Party (NEPP), Progressive People Alliance (PPA), and Republican Party of Nigeria (RPN). For a full list of parties with names of chairmen, national secretaries, treasurers, financial secretaries, and legal advisers, see *Nigeria Factbook*, 59ff.

Action Alliance (AA)

Advanced Congress of Democrats (ACD)

Alliance for Democracy (AD)

African Democratic Congress (ADC)

All Nigeria Peoples Party (ANPP)

Action Peoples Congress (APC)

All Progressives Grand Alliance (APGA)

All Peoples Liberation Party (APLP)

African Renaissance Party (ARP)

Better Nigeria Progressive Party (BNPP)

Community Party of Nigeria (CPN)

Citizens Popular Party (CPP)

Democratic Alternative (DA)

Fresh Democratic Party (FRESH)

Justice Party (JP)

Liberal Democratic Party of Nigeria (LDPN)

Labour Party (LP)

Movement for Democracy and Justice (MDJ)

Masses Movement of Nigeria (MMN)

Movement for the Restoration and Defence of Democracy (MRDD)

National Action Council (NAC)

Nigeria Advanced Party (NAP)

National Conscience Party (NCP)

New Democrats (ND)

National Democratic Party (NDP)

New Nigeria Peoples Party (NNPP)

Nigeria Peoples Congress (NPC)

National Reformation Party (NRP)

Progressive Action Congress (PAC)

Peoples Democratic Party (PDP)

Peoples Mandate Party (PMP)

Peoples Redemption Party (PRP)

Peoples Salvation Party (PSP)

United Democratic Party (UDP)

United Nigeria Peoples Party (UNPP)

The basic elements of a workable political system are in place in Nigeria, that is, a constitution that is not subject to the whims of incumbents and a multiparty system that is inclusive and apparently flexible enough to accommodate coalitions and alliances. The question is whether the electoral system can be free and fair, following the rule of law.[6]

Consolidating Rule of Law

Constitutional law is evolving in Nigeria and is the cornerstone of any national rule of law system.[7] Because of the British colonial heritage, with its "indirect rule" legacy of working through traditional political and legal systems, Nigeria has three main jurisprudential legs to its contemporary bench: British, Islamic, and "customary" (that is, non-Muslim indigenous cultural systems). Before independence in 1960, the Northern Region followed Islamic law in both criminal and civil domains. Historically, all of Muslim Africa has followed the Maliki school of Islamic jurisprudence, with a few exceptions among immigrant communities in East Africa. In Nigeria, Muslim law was applied only to Muslims during the colonial era. With independence, Nigeria shifted to a national system of laws in the criminal and corporate domains but permitted Islamic (sharia) law and customary law to serve in the civil domains as appropriate. Civil law (including marriage, divorce, inheritance) has been administered by a separate system of lower courts, with possibilities for appeal to higher levels. Both the 1979 and 1999 constitutions set out this multiple jurisprudential system in the civil domain.

The essence of rule of law is a level playing field, with equal justice for all. Laws should be transparent and available for reasoned interpretation in particular cases. In a federal system, states usually have the right to pass legislation, if not in conflict with constitutional law. Legal disputes between levels are settled through an appeals process up to a supreme court, which should be independent of those with political power.

In the election run-up to the Fourth Republic, a gubernatorial candidate (Ahmed Sani) from the northwest state of Zamfara ran on a platform of returning to sharia law in the criminal domain. He won, and in January 2000

---

6. On May 5, 2006, Professor Maurice Iwo, chairman of the Independent National Electoral Commission (INEC), reviewed election arrangements at a conference of the Nigerian People's Forum (NPF) in Washington, D.C. He emphasized the use of technology as a firewall against local corruption and welcomed international observers to the April 2006 elections. (The author chaired the panel on the constitutional framework at this conference.) Also, see "2007 Polls Hold April 7 to 29, Iwu Lists Steps to Credible Elections. Says No E-voting," http://www.gamji.com, May 25, 2006.

7. For background on constitutionalism in Africa, see Abdullahi Ahmed An-Na'im, *African Constitutionalism and the Role of Islam* (Philadelphia: University of Pennsylvania Press, 2006), especially chapter 5, "Islam and Constitutionalism in Sudan, Nigeria, and Senegal."

the Zamfara State assembly inaugurated legal reforms setting up sharia. After fifteen years of often capricious military rule, the sharia reforms were popular at the local level. Eleven other northern states followed suit and established sharia law in the criminal domain, making it applicable to Muslims only.[8]

After initial confusion and stress—and violent backlash in states such as Kaduna—the sharia systems in the northern states began to "normalize" in the Muslim communities. In the 2003 and 2007 elections, in part because of the need for national coalitions to cut across ethnoreligious and regional lines, the sharia controversy seemed to be less controversial. Some of the harsher punishments, such as stoning, had been overturned on appeal. Amputation for theft occurred in a few instances, but often because the defendants refused to pursue an appeals process. Yet, the sharia issue became a symbol of division within Nigeria. At the international level, there was widespread condemnation of the punishment and evidentiary aspects of sharia law in Nigeria, especially because women seemed to be more targeted.[9]

After the 2003 elections, and the success of the ANPP gubernatorial candidate in Kano, Ibrahim Shekarau, an alternative model to the Zamfara model emerged in the north. The Kano governor established three sharia bodies: the Sharia Commission, chaired by Sheikh Ibrahim Umar Kabo, the Hisbah board, chaired by Malam Abdullahi Muhammad Dutse, and the Zakat Commission, chaired by Muhammad Sani Zahradeen. In June 2005 the governor set up a fifty- member Shura Advisory Council, consisting of a wide range of distinguished religious scholars. Chaired by Sheikh Isa Waziri, the waziri of Kano, with Sheikh Na'ibi Sulaiman Wali as deputy chair, the council was to provide advice on religious matters and community affairs. In short, the governor has taken seriously the organizational and representational aspects of sharia. Governor Shekarau's overwhelming reelection in April 2007 confirmed the popularity of this approach.

---

8. Zamfara State of Nigeria, *Shari'ah Penal Code Law*, January 2000. Also, see Jibrin Ibrahim, ed., *Sharia Penal and Family Laws in Nigeria and in the Muslim World: Rights Based Approach* (Zaria: Global Rights, 2004). For background on classical roots of sharia in the Sokoto caliphate, see Shaykh Abdullahi B. Foduye, *Diya' al-Hukkam* [Guide to Administrators], edited and translated by Shehu Yamusa (Kano: 1975).

9. For a more detailed discussion of sharia in northern Nigeria after 2000, see John N. Paden, *Muslim Civic Cultures and Conflict Resolution: The Challenge of Democratic Federalism in Nigeria* (Washington, D.C.: Brookings Institution Press, 2005). Also, see Charlotte A. Quinn and Frederick Quinn, *Pride, Faith, and Fear: Islam in Sub-Saharan Africa* (New York, Oxford University Press, 2003), especially chapter 1, "Islam in Nigeria: Seeking a Competitive Edge." Also, see Benjamin F. Soares, ed., *Muslim-Christian Encounters in Africa*, especially chapter 9, Philip Ostien, "An Opportunity Missed by Nigeria's Christians: The 1976–78 Sharia Debate Revisited," and chapter 10, Franz Kogelmann, "The 'Sharia Factor' in Nigeria's 2003 Elections." Also, see Paul M. Lubeck, "Globalization, Democracy, and the 'Normalization' of the Shari'a Movement in Nigeria," presented at the Conference on Globalization, State Capacity and Muslim Movements, March 16–18, 2007, Washington, D.C.

Most important, the Kano model tries to avoid the emphasis on harsh punishment that many associate with the Zamfara model. Rather, the Kano approach aims to work with community leaders in restoring moral purpose, while focusing especially on training and employment of unemployed youth. The program also works with the more than twenty thousand Koranic and Islamiyya schools in Kano State to create practical educational opportunities and to provide moral instruction. Adherents of this model argue that the restoration of morals is mainly an educational endeavor, that education can contribute to preventing criminality, and that harsh penalties are not as effective a deterrent.[10] Within the Kano context, there has been a backlash against the so-called Wahhabi influence, and a conscious contrast with the so-called Zamfara model. The fact that the Kano and Zamfara governors are both members of the ANPP emphasizes that considerable variation exists within the twelve sharia states, including those with the same party affiliation.[11]

The larger issue within these twelve states is the relationship of Muslim and non-Muslim communities. Although alcohol and prostitution are generally illegal, regardless of religious affiliation, the method of implementing this ban varies widely. In some states strict constructionist Islamists have attacked beer parlors and hotels. In Kano, by contrast, Governor Shekarau has been working with the police to facilitate the ban, but without provocation.

Sharia law in Nigeria continues to be debated and evaluated. Of key importance is the critique that the law only applies to poor people (and/or women) and hence does not conform to the essence of rule of law, that is, equal treatment. In some states, such as Jigawa, this issue took the form of protests against the apparent exemption of royal family members from sharia law provisions. In most states—Kano has been an exception—corruption or embezzlement in office is not regarded as "theft" and hence has lighter punishments than ordinary stealing. During the 2003 elections in Zamfara, the PDP gubernatorial candidate criticized Governor Sani for using the law to punish the PDP and favor the ANPP. In short, perceived selective enforcement was the criterion for opposing "political sharia."

In spring 2006, the whole issue of *hisbah*, or volunteer neighborhood enforcers of sharia, became a national legal issue when the federal government took the Kano hisbah leaders to court for allegedly operating an ille-

---

10. In 2006, Bayero University, Kano, through its Centre for Democratic Research and Training (CDRT) based at Mambayya House, published a survey of more than six hundred Islamic scholars who had educational facilities in the north. The author is grateful to Haruna Waki-li, CDRT director, for making available a copy of this report.

11. In December 2006, Governor Ahmed Sani gave up his bid to run for president on the ANPP ticket but was elected senator on an ANPP ticket in April 2007 after his two-term limit as governor had ended.

gal security organization.[12] The Governor of Kano has vigorously defended the idea of hisbah at the state level.[13] As of spring 2007, with the elections pending, this issue had not been settled in the courts.

Meanwhile, at the national level, there have been several high profile cases of large-scale corruption, including the Inspector General (IG) of Police, who was alleged to have stolen $100 million. This case was dramatized in the media as the IG was recorded in handcuffs doing the perpetrator walk coming out of court on bail. (This larger issue of corruption is addressed below.) The question of who, if anyone, is above the law is a central issue in Nigeria and is related to the question of "immunity" for government officials from previous regimes.

The issue of sharia law is related to a larger challenge in Nigeria, that is, relations between religious communities. Given the tensions of transitioning to democratic federalism, the relationship of state laws to federal law (for example, states' rights to establish sharia) has yet to be tested in the national courts. As of 2007, none of the sharia criminal cases—other than the related issue of hisbah—had been taken to the Supreme Court, on which about half the judges are Muslim and half Christian.[14] The political implications are obvious as law takes on religious overtones.

More important, at the grassroots level, sharia law and interfaith relations have been used as symbols of confrontation, which, on occasion, have

12. See "Hisbah: Court Rules May 23 on Stay," *ThisDay*, May 17, 2006. Thus, "In February this year, Federal Government dragged the Chairman of Hisbah Corps, Yahaya Faruk Chedi, and his deputy, Abubakar Rabo Abdulkareen to court, charging them for allegedly conspiring to subvert the government by managing and assisting an unlawful society known as Hisbah Board Organization in Kano. Subsequently, the government of Kano State went to the Supreme Court of Nigeria asking it to determine the constitutionality of the Hisbah board. Kano State in the suit praying for an order stopping Federal Government from interfering with the implementation of the Hisbah laws in its domain, saying that the law establishing the Hisbah corps was validly passed by its House of Assembly. As a result of this suit, Federal Government has asked the Federal High Court Abuja to stay proceedings on the suit they filed against the Hisbah leaders pending the determination of the suit at the apex court."

13. See "Hisbah Leaders Are Heroes of Sharia—Shekarau," *ThisDay*, May 12, 2006. Thus, "Governor Ibrahim Shekarau of Kano State, has described leaders of the banned state security outfit, Hisbah, as heroes of Sharia. . . . Referred to as commanders, the suspects have been standing trial for allegedly operating an illegal security outfit. Shekarau commended them for their 'avowed bravery and commitment to the actualization of the truth in the midst of injustice and oppression.' He said the government and people would not despair and would continue with the struggle for the sustenance of the Islamic legal code in the state, and advised Hisbah officials to go about their normal duties within the confines of the laws of the land."

14. There are sixteen justices on the Supreme Court. Throughout most of the Fourth Republic the chief justice has been Muhammad Lawal Uwais of Zaria. After eleven years as chief justice and twenty-seven years on the bench, he retired at the mandatory age of seventy on June 12, 2006, and was replaced by Salihu Modibbo Alfa Belgore. He was subsequently replaced by Justice Idris Kutigi. Thus, as of 2007, the pattern is for the chief justice to be a northern Muslim. Also, in 2007, the appointed chair of the election reform commission was former chief justice Uwais, and the commission was balanced by representatives from throughout the country.

burst into real violence. Therefore, the question of how to manage, mediate, and even resolve conflict in Nigeria is another key challenge. Meanwhile, within the international context, Nigeria stands as one of six countries that allows stoning as a possible penalty in capital crimes (along with Saudi Arabia, Pakistan, Sudan, Yemen, and Iran).

Subsequent to the 2007 elections, the establishment of election tribunals and an election-reform commission seem to have quelled some of the fears that an independent judiciary would be intimidated by executive power. Indeed, in many quarters President Yar'Adua has been nicknamed "the rule-of-law president" because of his insistence that he will not interfere in court decisions.

The key to the stability and integrity of Nigeria depends on working across ethnoreligious cleavages. How sharia is interpreted and administered will be critical to the success of this multijurisprudential national experiment.

Developing Capacities for Conflict Resolution

Since the beginning of the Fourth Republic (1999), anywhere between ten thousand and sixty thousand civilians have been killed in local violent conflicts. The U.S.-based Human Rights Watch has issued empirically based reports on conflicts ranging from low-intensity insurgency in the oil-producing Delta areas to the so-called sharia riots in Kaduna (2000), the Miss World riots (2002), the tensions of political sharia, the mass killings of Muslims in Plateau State (2004), the revenge killings that followed in Kano (2004), and the killings and criminal activity associated with the 2007 elections. In 2006 Nigeria witnessed the highest number of killings of any country in the world—about 150—as a result of a Danish cartoon that was perceived as ridiculing the Prophet Muhammad.

Some of the violence associated with the 2003 elections has been mentioned above. In the April 2007 elections, European Union observers estimated that more than 230 people were killed. Human Rights Watch estimates that at least three hundred people were killed.[15] In addition, there have been serious clashes in secondary schools and universities over issues of religious symbolism. In September 2007, for example, students in Tudan Wada, Kano, engaged in deadly clashes that spread to the local community. In many local areas, militias have filled the gap in grassroots security, often outside the boundaries of the law. Although the underlying causes of such conflicts vary, their frequency and magnitude suggest a fundamental challenge to nation building in Nigeria.

The major means of dealing with such localized violence has been through the police and military, both of which are federal by constitutional

---

15. See "In Nigeria, Ballots Promise, but Bullets Rule," *New York Times*, October 10, 2007.

definition. The lack of a state and local police capability has often led to the military being called in to conflict situations, which usually exacerbates the tensions. While federal police are assigned to state and local duties, they may be out of touch with grassroots communities and may not even speak the local dialects.

Sometimes, as in Plateau State (2004), the police underreact and let local violence take its course. In other cases, as in Kano (2004), the police over-react and settle scores in an extrajudicial manner. Clearly, the first step in conflict mediation at the state and local levels is to develop police capabilities that are preventive rather than reactive and to move toward a commu-nity-based "serve and protect" model.

In addition, there are a range of social and cultural resources that could be mobilized. In many secondary schools and universities, interfaith peace committees serve as informal shock absorbers and mediators and stand ready to intercede in crisis situations. In addition, some non-governmen-tal organizations (NGOs)—including Academic Associates/PeaceWorks, which is based in Abuja but is active in the Delta and in the north, and the Inter-Faith Mediation Center, which is based in Kaduna and recently pro-duced a DVD film, *The Imam and the Pastor*—have provided valuable train-ing in conflict mediation and prevention. Such grassroots organizations are being encouraged and extended throughout the federation.[16]

The idea of a National Peace Council, with representatives from both Christian and Muslim communities, has been established in Abuja by the Obasanjo administration. Yet, the extension of such councils is most criti-cal at the state and local levels, where much of the violence transpires. A national council may send a symbolic message of conflict resolution, but it may be remote from the realities on the ground.

Much of the grassroots reality in Nigeria resides still in the unofficial domains of traditional rulers, also known as royal fathers. These emirs and chiefs have been transformed in the past forty years into symbolic spokes-men for local communities without any real executive powers. Yet their lifetime appointments (pending "good behavior") and roots in the commu-nities help them maintain back channel links with all local communities and put them in a position to communicate and mediate in potential crises. Most of the current generation of royal fathers are well educated and pro-

---

16. For discussion of the Kaduna mediation center, see David R. Smock, "Mediating between Christians and Muslims in Plateau State, Nigeria," in *Religious Contributions to Peacemak-ing: When Religion Brings Peace, Not War*, Peaceworks no. 55, ed. David R. Smock (Washing-ton, D.C.: United States Institute of Peace, January 2006), 17ff. Also, see Imam Muhammad Nurayn Ashafa and Pastor James Movel Wuye, "Training Peacemakers: Religious Youth Leaders in Nigeria," *Religious Contributions to Peacemaking*, 21ff. For background on AAPW, see issues of *PeaceWorks News*, newsletter of Academic Associates PeaceWorks, http://aa-peaceworks.org.

fessionally experienced. But they do not have the resources or tools, or the political imperative, to develop their potential as conflict mediators.[17]

This raises the question of whether professional training in conflict resolution methods and approaches should be offered as practical or academic courses of study. Some Nigerian universities, including Bayero University in Kano and Usman Dan Fodio Unversity in Sokoto are considering such instruction, but financial and professional incentives are needed.[18]

Finally, conflict resolution approaches are inevitably part of civic culture, the bedrock of democratic federalism. An overly centralized political system, perhaps inevitable in an oil-dependent country, requires specific initiatives to engage grassroots civil societies in the task of conflict mediation and resolution. During the military periods, there was a conscious attempt to separate political power from local cultures. Professional military officers often disdained the "backwardness" of traditional cultures. Yet most cultures have evolved ways to accommodate diversity and maintain harmony. While the circumstances have changed drastically since precolo-

---

17. For an editorial on the role of emirs and chiefs by the former editor of the *New Nigerian*, see Mahmud Jega, "The Sarkin Yaki's Beach-Head," December 1, 2005. Thus, "From the late 1960s right until the mid-1970s, the old institution of traditional rulership in Nigeria was in pell-mell constitutional retreat. Slowly they were stripped of the '*Yan Doka*, the once vaunted Native Authority police; then the courts were taken away, as were the prisons. And finally, in 1976, the entire Native Authority bureaucracy, complete with its treasury, was taken away from the chiefs. For the next 23 years or so, the traditional rulers' constitutional situation remained precarious but somewhat stable. At least the 1979 Constitution remembered to mention a Council of Chiefs at the state level as well as chairmen of the state Council of Chiefs as members of the Council of State, a fairly exalted kind of recognition. Even after the 1979 Constitution's violent overthrow, the ensuing military regimes largely maintained its spirit in so far as the chiefs were concerned. But in 1999 came the complete constitutional rout; a Constitution was promulgated into law that did not mention chiefs, even in passing, anywhere in its 160 pages.

"The strange thing though was this: four decades of full constitutional retreat by the royal fathers did not translate into a pell-mell political and social retreat by the institution. No state took a cue from the constitution and abolished the chiefs; instead, communities all over the country were demanding more and more chiefs of higher and higher grades and the governments were generally granting the requests."

18. There is considerable interest within Nigerian universities and training centers in conflict resolution. See, for example, H. Bobboyi and A. M. Yakubu, eds., *Peace-Building and Conflict Resolution in Northern Nigeria* (Kaduna: Arewa House, Centre for Historical Documentation and Research, Ahmadu Bello University, 2005). Also, see A. M. Yakubu, R. T. Adegboye, C. N. Ubah, B. Dogo, eds., *Crisis and Conflict Management in Nigeria since 1980*, vols. 1 and 2 (Kaduna: Nigerian Defence Academy, August, 2005). Also, Ibrahim Jumare and others, eds., *Nigeria: The Challenges of Peaceful Co-Existence* (Sokoto: December 2004). This three-day national conference, held at Usman Dan Fodio University, Sokoto, produced thirty-two working papers on such themes as root causes of conflicts in contemporary Nigeria; building bridges across religious and cultural divides; interethnic relations; conflict management strategies; role of education in peaceful coexistence; role of security organization in peaceful coexistence; and alternative frameworks for peaceful coexistence. The conference was opened by Tijjani Bande, vice chancellor of Usman Dan Fodio University, Governor Attiru Bafarawa, Sultan Muhammad Maccido, and a representative of President Obasanjo. In 2007, the Centre for Peace Studies, under the office of the vice-chancellor, was established at Usman Dan Fodio University. (Note: the proper name is Usmanu Danfodiyo University but has been standardized in this monograph to reflect the name of the Sokoto founder.)

nial times, some of the essential cultural components can be rediscovered and reformed to serve contemporary circumstances. Democratic federalism will fail or succeed depending on the extent to which ordinary people are engaged in the endeavor, and this means working with the best of the local values.

Without peace at the local level, prosperity is illusory. Violent conflicts prevent economic development from both the domestic and international perspective. Some form of peace and stability is a precondition for economic development. This requires a workable political system at all levels, consolidation of rule of law, and capacities for conflict resolution. Most clearly, it requires leadership, at both the state and regional or national levels.[19] Then the major tasks of economic development can be undertaken. A nation cannot fight poverty while violence abounds.

Facilitating Economic Development

The often unstated premise of economic development in Nigeria is that all thirty-six states in the federation should have equal opportunity in terms of access to educational, economic, and political participation. The principle of federal character has been enshrined in all constitutions since 1979, but in practice it was also the premise of the First Republic (1960–66). The Northern Region, with its demographic predominance but relative disadvantage in terms of access to modern education and jobs, developed a policy of "northernization" to catch up with the more westernized south. While this policy was politically controversial in Nigeria at the time, it evolved in a way that is now widely accepted—that is, that no state or region should be left behind in the development process. The oil-driven economy has made possible a more evenhanded geographic approach to development, although the question of access to oil revenues continues to be a central political issue.

---

19. See "Cartoon Riot: Hausa Community Commends Ibori on Assistance," *Sunday Independent*, April 2006. For a different view, see "Religious Riots: Govs, Security Agents Blamed for High Tolls," *ThisDay*, May 11, 2006. See also "Northern Students Flay Religious Conflicts," *ThisDay*, April 4, 2006. Thus, "The National Association of Northern Nigerian Students (NANNS) yesterday said it had concluded arrangements to mount intensive campaign aimed at sensitizing Nigerians on the dangers of religious intolerance. In a statement signed by its President, Mallam Mohammed Usman, NANNS said decision to mount the campaign was taken at a meeting in Maiduguri, Borno State, on April 5, 2006. It said participants at the meeting agreed that frequent religious conflicts posed threat to the unity and progress of the country and identified the need for Northern Nigerian students to take the lead in sensitizing and re-orientating Nigerians on the implications of religious conflict. 'We recognized the pain, trauma and agony frequent religious conflicts have caused Nigerians. We decided to mount campaigns against religious conflict as a way of curbing the phenomenon.' The campaign with the theme, 'Operation make Nigeria free of religious conflicts' and sub-theme, 'Religious tolerance, an inevitable ingredient for national unity and socio-economic development,' would be inaugurated by the Minister of Education, Mrs. Chinwe Obaji, in Abuja."

A key to the federal-character approach—as part of power sharing —is the constitutional provision regarding land use, which stipulates that all land is "crown land" (in the British tradition).[20] Subsoil minerals (including oil) are the heritage of all Nigerians and not simply those sitting on the land. This allows the federal government to allocate oil revenues back to the states (according to constitutional formulae) in the form of block grants. It also allows state governments to allocate land for "use" (that is, rights of usufruct) rather than outright ownership. State and local authorities issue certificates of occupancy. Rights of eminent domain, therefore, are implicit in this principle. Clearly, this policy is a double-edged sword. It allows for equal access but also opens the door to favoritism and corruption.

The dependence on oil revenues in the federal budget has produced a mono-crop mentality in that government (at all levels) is perceived to be the major employer in the country. Access to jobs, especially for university graduates, is partly a matter of merit, partly a matter of state affiliation, and partly a matter of political connections. This did not change much during the Obasanjo administration's policy of privatization, except to fuel northern fears that southerners would dominate in both the private and public domains. The political demands in the south-south—that oil revenue distributions be recalibrated to favor these states—has already produced a backlash in the north. If taken to extremes, the demands of south-south politicians and/or insurgency groups may contribute more than any other factor to undermining the national unity of the country.

Also at the macroeconomic level, the relative lack of financial-service institutions and capacity has produced a cash-and-carry mentality. Because of the current concern in the global economy with terrorism and the role of transferable funds across international boundaries, the Obasanjo administration restricted many smaller banks and consolidated the ninety or so established banks into about twelve to twenty-five larger institutions so they could be more easily regulated. But the underdeveloped nature of financial services in Nigeria has limited internal development, encouraged savings abroad, and created a climate of trying to avoid bureaucratic regulation, which at a minimum adds another layer of cost to any business calculation.[21]

However, one of the new banks to be licensed by the Central Bank in Nigeria is Ja'iz Bank, the first interest-free bank in Nigeria. And Governor

---

20. For background on land use law in Nigeria, see Karol C. Boudreaux, "The Human Face of Resource Conflict: Property and Power in Nigeria," *San Diego International Law Journal* 7, no. 1 (Fall 2005). For a journalistic discussion of oil and land issues in the Delta, see Lisa Margonelli, *Oil on the Brain: Adventures from the Pump to the Pipeline* (New York: Doubleday, 2007), especially chapter 10, "Calling the Warlord's Cell Phone."

21. For a discussion of economic institutional building, see Peter M. Lewis, *Growing Apart: Oil, Politics, and Economic Change in Indonesia and Nigeria* (Ann Arbor: University of Michigan Press, 2007).

Ahmed Sani announced in July 2005 that Nigeria had registered Ja'iz Bank with the Islamic Development Bank, a broad umbrella financial network headquartered in Kuala Lumpur, Malaysia. Hence, Nigeria currently is in the Islamic banking business.

The political uncertainties in Nigeria during the oil boom and bust cycles have also resulted in large-scale human capital flight. Millions of Nigerians—middle class and professional, as well as semiskilled and un-skilled—are living and working abroad, not only in the United States and the United Kingdom but also throughout Africa and elsewhere. Remit-tances to families in Nigeria, through various means, have become a major nonvisible source of support to many extended families. Since educated, middle-class sectors of society are critical to establishing a workable politi-cal system, consolidating rule of law, and developing capacities for conflict mediation, the role of the Nigerian diaspora has an exponential impact on the economy, both by its domestic absence and its overseas potential for human and financial capital.[22]

During the military periods, many of the Nigerians who went overseas were from the south. Whether they will return during the Fourth Republic with their talents and resources is an open question. What impact they will have on the delicate political and economic balance between regions in Nigeria will have profound effects. In short, Nigerians from all regions have become globalized in terms of their aspirations and abilities to function within a world context. Yet, if capital returns to Nigeria from abroad, especially as state resources are privatized, this may reinforce a sense of class and regional dominance among ordinary Nigerians.

At the grassroots level, there are three major economic issues: jobs, edu-cational opportunities, and health-and-welfare concerns. The Shekarau administration in Kano is trying to combine job training and educational opportunities not only in the modern, English-speaking sector but also in the informal, non–English speaking sectors. And the Islamiyya schools are attempting to combine Islamic basics with modern fields such as science and history.

In general, the educational structures in Nigeria were modeled on British patterns. In the past, this meant that higher education was more focused on elites, and all levels tended to avoid practical training, whether in technology or business. A recent exception of this is the new private Abti Univeristy in Yola (Adamawa State), commonly known as the American University, Yola,

---

22. See "Foreign-based Nigerians Repatriate $12bn Annually," *Businessday,* May 17, 2006, 6, which noted, "Nigerians in the diaspora inject about $12 billion into the economy annu-ally, the President of the Nigerian Information Technology Professionals in the Americas, Prof. Manny Aniebonam, has disclosed. . . . Aniebonam estimated that about 6.5 million Nigerians were residing in North America with about 197,000 of them engaged in lucrative information and communications technology (ICT) vocations."

which was sponsored by Atiku Abubakar and is based on an American model with an emphasis on practical skills, such as technology and entrepreneurship. Yet, the fluctuation of oil revenues has meant uncertainty about resources for education at any given time. And while universities have produced tens of thousands of graduates, sometimes under trying circumstances, graduates ask, where are the jobs? In the Muslim north, the phenomenon of unemployed or underemployed university graduates, or dropouts, has been a challenge in both the socioreligious and economic domains.[23]

Likewise, the health-and-welfare concerns, which were often handled by extended families in the past, are fast becoming a matter for religious organizations. Christian storefront churches, often with evangelical or Pentecostal leanings, abound in the south and in every northern city. The practice of faith healing is commonplace, as is the reliance on prayer in the search for jobs and prosperity. In the Muslim communities, the Sufi brotherhoods once provided some of these services. Increasingly, resources of wealthy Nigerian Muslims throughout the country are being used to support charities, mosques, and schools, and especially the poor.

Economic development, if it is to go beyond trickle-down oil revenues, must take account of the social and political realities in Nigeria. Normally, this is where democratic federalism can create incentives for local initiatives if overcentralization and bureaucratic mismanagement can be contained. Nigerians are known for their vibrant entrepreneurship and agricultural skill, but how to harness this legacy to the new realities of a globalizing economy is a challenge for the Nigerian leadership at all levels.

Detailed accounts of the Nigerian oil industry are not possible here, except to note that the oil industry itself is normally transparent in terms of crude oil produced officially and prices paid. Yet the unofficial misdirection of oil from local producing sites and its offshore sale (known as bunkering) by high-level officials are serious problems. Because much of Nigerian refined oil has to be reimported by the Nigerian National Petroleum Corporation (NNPC) and is then sold at state-regulated prices (well below market levels), the state is losing money. The federal Petroleum Products Pricing and Regulatory Agency (PPRA) complained in July 2005 that more than thirty million liters of fuel are consumed every day, and that even if Nigerian refineries were working at full capacity, which, at best, means 80 percent, they could only meet 50 percent of local consumption.

Meanwhile, ordinary Nigerians demand low fuel prices as their right (and one of their few direct benefits) in an oil-producing state, even if it

---

23. As an example, in 2006–07, Bayero University, Kano, had a total of 27,264 students, of which 6,376 were in sciences, 1,658 in technology, 620 in medicine, and 4,793 in education. Yet, jobs are still scarce, even for well-qualified applicants.

means large state subsidies. Local riots and turmoil have resulted when the government has tried to raise the price of gas at the pump. The government counters that subsidized fuel prices means that supplies will be traded illegally to other countries in West Africa paying international prices for oil.

The international financial institutions have tried to help upgrade Nigeria's energy-sector capacity. In July 2005 the World Bank increased its annual budget for Nigeria from $200 million to $500 million, including $172 million to support the energy sector and facilitate new market and institutional structural energy-sector reform.

Finally, it is a challenge to create the conditions for constructive foreign direct investment in Nigeria, from whatever sources. Since the passage of the U.S. Foreign Corrupt Practices Act in 1977, there has been relatively little U.S. investment in Nigeria outside of the oil sector. But British and European investment in Nigeria has not abated. By early 2005 Nigeria owed about $30 billion to international creditors, of which only about $1 billion was to U.S. banks. In July 2005 the Paris Club granted debt relief of about $18 billion and urged that the money be invested in the country's physical and human infrastructure, in agriculture, and in reducing the level of poverty. In spring 2006, after much negotiation, $12 billion was paid by Nigeria to the Paris Club to cancel its major debts.

More recently, China has become involved in investments in Nigeria, as elsewhere in Africa.[24] In June 2005, for example, Chinese companies announced investments in Ogun State to establish a furniture village in the Ijebu East local government area. The overall relationship between China and Nigeria is described by Lawal M. Marafa:[25]

> This is the second time that President Obasanjo and entourage are arriving in Beijing. . . . The benefits of such visits should be able to trickle down to the populace. In the first visit of a Chinese leader to Nigeria . . . President Jiang Zemin in April 2002 expressed the need for furtherance of bilateral relations and need to work on common ground on both regional and international issues. . . . It is no secret that China seeks to pursue an investment drive in Africa. As China attempts to diversify its investment potential and court new markets, high-level visits to Africa have

24. See Bates Gill, Chin-hao Huang, and J. Stephen Morrison, *China's Expanding Role in Africa: Implications for the United States,* report of the CSIS delegation to China on China-Africa-U.S. Relations, November 28–December 1, 2006 (Washington, D.C.: Center for Strategic and International Studies, January 2007). Appendix 1 contains the report of the "Forum on China-Africa Cooperation: Beijing Action Plan (2007–2009)," based on the November 3–5, 2006, Beijing Summit and the Third Ministerial Conference of the Forum on China-Africa Cooperation (FOCAC). The Nigerian president and at least forty high-ranking Nigerian cabinet officers attended.

25. "China and Nigeria: Seeking Partnership and a Symbiotic Relationship," April 12, 2005, www.AmanaOnline.

become commonplace. . . . While it is clear that China is now in the vanguard of tapping investment opportunities in Africa, Nigeria as a leading country in the continent should go into bi-lateral relationships with clear interests that will be able to be measured by the extent of deliverability.

In April 2006, President Hu Jintao of China visited Abuja, and discussions were held on a wide range of commercial projects, including those dealing with the oil industry. Clearly, China will become more involved in Nigerian business ventures.[26]

Yet, the key to future investment may well be the prospect of returning Nigerian "flight capital" and overseas accumulated capital, which by some calculations may be over $100 billion. As in China (where the overseas Chinese are still the major FDI investors), the ambivalence of overseas Nigerians to put their lives and money at risk is balanced by the "local knowledge" factor and the pull of family ties. Yet, the cost of doing business in Nigeria, even for Nigerian expatriates, is compounded by the perception that corruption is rampant at all levels and politics are never stable.

International factors have also influenced the emphasis on economic reforms at the federal level in Nigeria, as was made clear when Ngozi Okonjo-Iweala, a World Bank economist, returned to be finance minister.[27]

---

26. According to a U.S. Congressional Research Service (CRS), Library of Congress, report, *China and Sub-Saharan Africa* (August 29, 2005), "In Nigeria the China Civil Engineering Construction Corporation is rehabilitating the nation's dilapidated railway system, and Nigeria has purchased a Chinese-built communications satellite, which China Aerospace plans to launch in 2007. The satellite agreement was reached during an April 2005 visit to Beijing by Nigeria's President Olusegun Obasanjo. During the visit, the two countries also agreed that a Chinese firm would introduce wireless telephone service into Nigeria's rural areas, and that they would upgrade their relationship to a 'strategic partnership' with enhanced cooperation in trade, investment, and agriculture. Agreements have been reported on the purchase of Chinese-manufactured jet fighters and trainers for the Nigerian Air Force. Meanwhile, Chinese-produced motorcycles are reportedly flooding the Nigerian market. Many are locally assembled, and a Chinese firm is negotiating to set up a plant to manufacture parts locally.

   "Energy appears to be the key motivator of China's relationship with oil-rich Nigeria, and Chinese firms are engaged in oil and gas exploration there, as well as in providing technical services to the oil industry. In July 2005, Petro-China International negotiated a deal for the importation of 30,000 barrels of Nigerian oil per day over five years. The company had earlier secured a license to operate in four of Nigeria's oil blocks, and in exchange is building a Nigerian hydro-power station."

27. Okonjo-Iweala remained in Nigeria only until 2006, however. See "Rebuilding a Life and Then a Country," *Washington Post*, May 10, 2006. Thus, "It fell to Ngozi Okonjo-Iweala, barely 13 at the start of the Nigeria-Biafra war, to save her baby sister, struck down with malaria. . . . Okonjo-Iweala is no stranger to heavy burdens, and today, at age 51, she has a new one: She is the first female finance minister in Nigeria, and in Africa. In that role, she has overseen an opening up of finances in a corruption-ridden country and the paying off of billions of dollars in debt." In 2006, Okonjo-Iweala resigned as finance minister and became foreign minister. Later that year, she resigned that post and returned to the international community sector and family matters. In 2007 she became managing director of the World Bank.

In addition, President Obasanjo did play a key role within the international community in trying to attract interest and resources for economic development in Africa, including in the agricultural domains.[28]

Yet issues of economic reform are clearly related to issues of corruption. In 2000, Transparency International, in its corruption perception index, ranked Nigeria as the most corrupt country in the world. Subsequently, Nigeria has trended in the right direction. After placing in the top three along with Haiti and Bangladesh, Nigeria was ranked 152 out of 159 countries in 2005, a slight improvement.[29] And in 2007, it was ranked the thirty-second most corrupt nation.

Anyone who has tried to function in Nigeria, including citizens and noncitizens, knows the meaning of the word "dash," which may also be interpreted as a user's fee or facilitation fee. (The Hausa word, *goro*, is also used, referring to a kola nut, which is often given as a gift.) The U.S. Foreign Corrupt Practices Act regards facilitation fees, even if not known to higher-level executives, to be illegal and subject to U.S. court action. This issue joins the short list of the challenges of nation building in Nigeria and is clearly related to the previous four issues.

Stemming Corruption at All Levels

There are three obvious approaches to fighting corruption in Nigeria: encouraging official will and action, establishing leadership by example, and engaging civic cultures.

Official will and action were undertaken aggressively by the Buhari military regime (1984–85), and many senior politicians and businessmen were sent to jail for long terms. But within less than two years, Buhari was overthrown by the Babangida military regime, which took a more relaxed view, and most high-level prisoners were released. When Sani Abacha came to power in 1993, the massive looting of the federal treasury continued. In the Fourth Republic era, some of the approximately $3 billion of Abacha money in Swiss banks has been returned to Nigeria. Yet, as of 2006, the Nigerian government was still demanding that $458 million of Abacha money in

---

28. See "Overfarming African Land Is Worsening Hunger Crisis," *New York Times*, March 31, 2006, which quotes from a news conference held by the Nigerian leader: "The degradation of farmland across sub-Saharan Africa has accelerated at an ominous rate over the past decade, deepening a hunger crisis that already afflicts more than 250 million Africans. . . . 'To feed our people, we must feed our soils,' said Nigeria's president Olusegun Obasanjo, at a news conference at the Rockefeller Foundation in New York City. . . . Obasanjo will be the host of a June meeting on Africa's fertilizer needs in Abuja that is expected to draw leading experts on rural development as well as wealthy donors."

29. See "Nigeria, Corruption and Transparency International," *Guardian* (Lagos and Abuja), editorial, November 8, 2005.

Swiss banks be returned to fight poverty, support agriculture, and build infrastructure.

In 2005 the second Obasanjo administration began to crack down on high-level corruption. The high profile case of the arrest and conviction of the Inspector General of Police—for stealing $100 million—sent a message that even the highest officials are not above the law.[30] The question as to how far back to look for irregularities is clearly a political issue, since much of the money used in the 2003 and 2007 elections has come from unknown sources.

In 2004, an Economic and Financial Crimes Commission (EFCC) and Independent Corrupt Practices Commission (ICPC) had been set up and began to examine high-level cases more carefully.[31] The young lawyer who is chair of EFCC, Nuhu Ribadu (originally from Yola), is quite active in trying to pursue cases.[32] In some instances, he appeared to be held back by the office of the president, given the political sensitivities of many cases. For instance, in July 2005 Obasanjo described corruption allegations against former military leader Ibrahim Babangida as "unsubstantiated coffee shop rumors." Yet, Ribadu has also been criticized as being too close to the dominant political powers, especially during the 2007 election cycle. (He has continued his probes of former governors following the 2007 election.)

The alleged bribes paid to National Assembly legislators in an attempt to influence the third-term decision in May 2006 probably goes beyond what the EFCC can address. In 2006 there were indications that Ribadu might bring specific corruption charges against many of the governors when their

---

30. See "Will Tafa Be Tried?" *Vanguard,* December 1, 2005. Thus, "The anti-corruption crusade of this administration dipped slightly November 22, 2005, when an Abuja Federal High Court sentenced Alhaji Adebayo Mustafa Balogun, erstwhile Inspector General of Police, to a four-year jail term. It actually transpired that he would not spend more than SIX months in jail since the sentence would run concurrently and his period of detention was to be discounted."

31. For background on EFCC and ICPC, see *Economic and Financial Crimes Commission (Establishment Act)* (2004); President Obasanjo, "Special Address" to Economic and Financial Crimes Commission, 1st Executive Session on Corruption, Abuja, August, 6, 2005; *Economic and Financial Crimes Commission, Money Laundering (Prohibition Act)* (2004); Osita Nwajah, *The EFCC Story* (Abuja: EFCC, n.d.); and Economic and Financial Crimes Commission, Nigeria, *Zero Tolerance* 1, no. 1 (July 2006).

32. See Nuhu Ribadu, chairman of the Economic and Financial Crimes Commission, "Nigeria's Struggle with Corruption," presentation to the U.S. House Committee on International Relations, Subcommittee on Africa, Global Human Rights and International Operations, Washington, D.C., May 18, 2006. Chairman Ribadu discusses the EFCC anticorruption strategy, describes the EFCC, assesses positive results so far (including taking action against terrorist financing, setting up machinery for monitoring activities in the oil industry, and making efforts against Internet scams and identity theft), discusses relationships with law enforcement authorities (including international units), and assesses what remains to be done.

In December, 2007, Ribadu was "reassigned" to a year-long course at the Nigerian Institute of Policy and Strategic Studies (NIPSS). Rumors swirled as to whether he would resign, which caused concern among those who feared a weakening of the anti-corruption probes. In January 2008, President Yar'Adua approved the appointment of Ibrahim Lamorde as acting chair of EFCC. Lamorde was the EFCC Director of Operations and also came from Adamawa state.

terms expired and they were no longer immune.[33] The case of the arrest and impeachment of the governor of Bayelsa State in 2005 is a major symbol of cooperation between the international community and the EFCC.[34]

Also, in 2005 the results of the Oputa Commission—a human rights violations investigations commission headed by Justice Chukwudifu Oputa—were given to the NPRC for consideration. The report recommended that all past military rulers be disbarred from future political office. This was a clear slap at General Ibrahim Babangida, but it would also have affected Muhammadu Buhari. It was seen as an attempt to disqualify most prominent northerners from future office if they had served under previous military administrations.

With regard to leadership by example, clearly Buhari stands out as the most prominent political figure who has taken a hard-line against high-level corruption and has tried to behave in such a way as to be above reproach. During the heat of the 2003 and 2007 elections, there was no allegation of financial impropriety by Buhari, who symbolizes a modest, unostentatious lifestyle. Yet Buhari's image as "Mr. Clean" seemed to work against his chances to prevail in the real world of Nigerian politics: his campaign was chronically short of funds, and many political activists expected some sort of remuneration. Significantly, Umaru Yar'Adua was also associated with a clean record as governor of Katsina, which may have been a factor in his selection as PDP candidate for president in December 2006. With his election in 2007, Yar'Adua declared his assets at $5 million, which is considered modest by Nigerian political standards.

Without clear examples of strict financial propriety at the highest levels, others in the political and business milieu are unlikely to set new leadership examples. Many of those who might serve as the best examples of influential persons have removed themselves from the Nigerian business or political arenas. Yet the lack of such leadership in Nigeria is a clear disincentive to future generations of potential leaders and a source of enormous frustration and anger at the level of ordinary citizens. The nature of the Nigerian economy makes it very easy to cut corners when it comes to the old-fashioned virtues of honesty and integrity. It is within this context

---

33. See *Daily Independent*, June 13, 2006, which claims that as many as twenty-four governors may face corruption charges in 2007 when they leave office. The list is reported as "secret."

34. See "As Nigeria Tries to Fight Graft, A New Sordid Tale: Antics of a Governor Reinforce Nation's Image as Corrupt," *New York Times*, November 29, 2005. Also, see "Nigeria Arrests Runaway Governor: A Nigerian State Governor Who Was Charged with Money Laundering in the UK Has Been Impeached and Arrested in His Oil-Rich Home State of Bayelsa," BBC News, December 9, 2005. Thus, "Diepreye Alamieyeseigha was detained by police after losing the immunity from prosecution that he enjoyed in office. He has always said he is innocent of charges that he laundered 1.8 million pounds ($3.2m) found in cash and bank accounts. As Nigeria battles to shed a reputation for corruption, this is the first time a governor has been impeached."

that a grassroots return to traditional values, including Islamic values, is taking place.

The real engagement of civil society may be an antidote to some of the amoral realities of the political and business world in Nigeria, although even civil society is not immune from the culture of corruption.[35] Certainly in the Muslim areas, the return to sharia may have opened a Pandora's box of expectations, especially with regard to embezzlement and financial malfeasance. Civil society in the north is already asking questions such as, if a cattle thief should have a hand amputated, what about a civil servant who gives contracts to an unqualified relative, or a departmental minister who cooks the books to his own advantage? In short, the spirit of sharia is about justice and integrity, quite apart from the strict fundamentals of punishments and the literal interpretations of classical texts. Within the areas of the nineteenth-century Sokoto caliphate, the return to the examples of the founding fathers—the "Shehu" (Usman Dan Fodio), his brother (Abdullahi), and son (Muhammad Bello), plus early examples of learned and pious women from the Dan Fodio family (for example, the daughter of the Shehu, Nana Asma'u)—has created a dynamic tension between classical ideals and contemporary realities.

---

35. See Daniel Jordan Smith, *A Culture of Corruption: Everyday Deception and Popular Discontent in Nigeria* (Princeton: Princeton University Press, 2007). Of special interest, see "'God Is in Charge': The Popularity of Pentecostal Christianity," 207ff, in which he notes how many preachers criticize corruption in sermons but have no hesitation in using every means possible to acquire wealth. His major focus is in the Igbo-speaking southeast zone.

4

Pathways of Change

This chapter will examine the politics of alternative futures, including the Shell Oil "Vision 2010" scenarios, political perspectives on worst-case scenarios, and political turnover prospects. In addition, it will focus on power-sharing and power-shifting aspects of the 2007 election, including an assessment of the electoral process, the religious balance factor in Nigerian politics, Fourth Republic power-sharing and power-shifting, postelection reactions, the legitimating role of traditional emirs and chiefs in northern Nigeria, and the challenges ahead. Finally, it will assess pathways of political change, such as partitioning, centralization, and democratic federalism. Nigerian pathways of change are notoriously difficult to project. The adage "expect the unexpected" is almost a national motto. Yet the parameters of change are clearly apparent, and having ridden the boom and bust cycles of an oil economy since the 1970s, Nigerians have come to accept that no condition is permanent.

The Politics of Alternative Futures for Nigeria

Scenarios are projected alternative futures based on imagination and discipline. They are not predictions. In some cases probabilities may be estimated. The purpose of scenarios is to create an awareness of possible future events and a sense of lateral vision so that planners are not blind-sided by the unexpected. Most governments, large corporations, and even academic institutions engage in some form of scenario planning.

The art of scenario planning was developed after World War II, especially by the Shell Oil Corporation, as a way to project ten to fifteen years into the future because of the lead time necessary for oil exploration, extraction, and pipeline construction. Factors of political, economic, and social conditions were critical to the oil industry. Specialized units within Shell Oil combined the art of storytelling with highly technical quantitative simulations. Each story required that key factors be identified and weighted. In general, the alternative scenarios could be seen as the good, the bad, and the ugly. By using the scenario approach, Shell Oil was one of the few corporations to have anticipated the Arab oil boycott of 1973 and to have positioned itself accordingly. In today's world, Shell Oil has scenario plans for each country in which it does significant business, including Nigeria. Shell draws heavily on the work of scholars such as Peter Schwartz and Kees van der Heijden and is highly interactive with business and political planners in each country.[1]

Some scenarios are short term (three years). Some are medium (ten to fifteen years) or long term (twenty-five years). Alternative outcomes are projected as a way of sensitizing decision makers to avoid tunnel vision and the tendency to make linear and incremental projections from the present and to encourage the recognition of possible nonlinear change.

The Shell Oil "Vision 2010" Scenarios for Nigeria

In 1996 Shell Oil projected fourteen-year scenarios for Nigeria.[2] The twenty-five-page public report was prepared for the Nigerian Economic Summit in September 1996. Subsequently, these scenarios were presented to the Vision 2010 conference in which several hundred Nigerian political and business leaders (including traditional royal fathers, business executives, civil servants, former military officers, former civilian office holders, senior academics, and others) met in Abuja in January 1997. "Vision 2010" refers to economic projections in Nigeria to the year 2010. The author was an observer at this conference.

The Vision 2010 conference was also significant in drawing together leaders from all parts of the federation and was approximately balanced between Muslims and Christians. In terms of ambiance, the conference began and ended with Muslim and Christian prayers. The keynote speaker was a Muslim economist from Malaysia. The scenario facilitators tended to be British (some ethnically Chinese) from London. The conference provided an opportunity for Nigerian cross-regional (and hence interfaith) interactions and possible alliances.

Shell projected that the factors of liberalization, globalization, and technology would result in an overarching condition of "There Is No Alternative" (TINA). Within this approach there were two paths to a successful society: "Da Wo" (that is, "Big We" in Chinese), with its long-term vision, cohesive social values, and emphasis on social democracy, and "Just Do It," with its emphasis on hypercompetition, free-market liberalism, and individualism. A third alternative scenario was the "Road to Kinshasa," in which societies were based on strife, with beleaguered dictatorships, minimum social control, the economics of isolation, and the tearing of the social fabric.

The TINA option of Just Do It assumes one global economy in the future with individual countries opting to be in or out. The global economy would be market driven, and the governments would be increasingly democratic. Private-sector initiatives would be the key to this scenario.

---

1. See Peter Schwartz, *The Art of the Long View* (New York: Doubleday, 1991) and Kees van der Heijden, *Scenarios: The Art of Strategic Conversation* (New York: Wiley, 1996).
2. Vincent Cable, *Nigerian Scenarios, 1996–2010* (Shell Oil, 1996).

The Big We scenario also assumes a global economy but allows for more of a communitarian (rather than individualistic) approach. Some of the socialist market economies, such as China, fit this model.

The third scenario, the Road to Kinshasa, is obviously a metaphor for a declining or failing state. Kinshasa refers to the current Democratic Republic of Congo, which has rich natural resources but a weak and ineffective government. Furthermore, it has little national unity and is plagued by civil wars and localized strife. The Kinshasa option assumes that the country is not well connected to the global economy.

After several days of discussion, the Shell Oil presenters asked the participants to vote as to which scenario was most likely for Nigeria. The overwhelming majority of participants chose TINA/Just Do It. A few chose Big We, and none chose the Road to Kinshasa. Clearly, there was a prevailing optimism in Nigeria among these opinion leaders, even at a time when the Abacha regime was cracking down on dissent and stifling foreign direct investment. Participants, especially from the stressed business community, expected that eventually Nigeria would be democratic, market driven, and part of the global economy.

With the return to civilian rule in 1999, many in the Nigerian leadership anticipated that the TINA/Just Do It scenario would prevail. A "democracy dividend," a privatization initiative, and a vibrant oil economy all seemed to portend a bright future. Cross-regional alliances were in place to take advantage of these opportunities.

Yet other realities soon began to intrude on Vision 2010. The mono-crop economy of oil seemed to pull toward a government-dominant system. The end of the military era, with its strict sociopolitical controls, seemed to portend intense zonal or regional competition. Ethnoreligious conflict in Kaduna and Plateau states (plus reverberating echoes in other states), turmoil in the Delta, the extraordinary gap between new wealth and grassroots poverty (often fueled by corruption), and the widespread perception in the north that power had shifted unduly to the southwest combined into an atmosphere of suspicion and perceived grievances. Could the center hold? Could it hold if the decentralization so essential to federalism was not achieved? The election of 2003, in which incumbent rigging was widely alleged, seemed to intensify these concerns. Could Nigeria be on the Road to Kinshasa and not know it? Would this result in ethnoreligious factionalism that could threaten the federation?

On the political front, as the summer of 2005 unfolded, there was the deadlock at the National Political Reform Conference (NPRC). In addition, the census in March 2006 was of concern in many quarters because of uncertainty about power reallocation and possible ethnoreligious implications. The campaigns by presidential hopefuls in all political parties were in high gear, with resultant tensions. Some governors announced that if the census did not ac-

curately reflect their perceived demographic strengths, they would not accept the results. Dominating these apprehensions was the unresolved issue of
whether political incumbents could manipulate an extension of their terms.
The scenario of Just Do It seemed to assume a more stable political environment than was emerging in Nigeria.

Political Perspectives on Worst-Case Scenarios

The United States had already considered a worst-case scenario for Nigeria
in a report of January 2005 released by the U.S. National Intelligence Council
(NIC). (At the time, these internal reports were made available publicly on
the Internet. This policy has changed subsequently.) The report was put on
the Internet in March and picked up by the Nigerian media. (Many Nigerians
assumed the report was leaked because they were not aware of the NIC's
transparency policy at the time.) The "worst-case" scenario caused a political
firestorm in Nigeria. According to Nigerian accounts, it estimated that
within fifteen years Nigeria would not survive as a country. Was the U.S.
really projecting that Nigeria would follow the Road to Kinshasa and
actually fail as a state?[3]

Some of the critics of the Obasanjo administration took an "I told you so"
position. Others argued that the warning flag was up and Nigeria should address these problems rather than go into denial. President Obasanjo is reported to have described the U.S. report as "glib talk." Still others took the view
that "America has clearly set out to undermine Nigeria, to create instability
and disintegration."[4]

According to Abdulrazaque Bello-Barkindo, a respected journalist, the report "must not be taken as lightly as our garrulous power-mongers are already doing. . . . The report, we all know is and cannot be the gospel truth, just
as it's by no means a prophecy or prediction but a summary of a collection of
information available to the US body and a wake-up call for the country. But
reactions to the report since its release in Nigeria have been anything but edi-
fying with the most brazen coming from the president who himself described
it as mere 'glib talk.'"[5]

President Obasanjo forwarded the report to members of the Nigerian Senate in May 2005. The Senate Foreign Relations Committee took the NIC report
seriously and set up a special ad hoc committee. Many political leaders wor-

---

3. See, for example, "Why Nigeria May Become a Failed State . . . How to Salvage the Situ-
    ation," *Vanguard*, June 3, 2005; Obadiah O. Alegbe, "The American Prediction of Fifteen
    Years to the Fall of Nigeria Must Not Be Ignored" (oghoerore@oviri.com.ar) May 31, 2005;
    "Regard U.S. Security Report as a Challenge, Makarfi Tells Nigerians," *Daily Independent*,
    May 31, 2005; Afenifeer, "How to Prevent Nigeria's Break-up, by Afenifere," *Daily Indepen-
    dent*, May 31, 2005.
4. See Paul Adujie, "America Means Well for Nigeria: Oh Really?" AmanaOnline,
    June 30, 2005.
5. AmanaOnline, July 11, 2005.

ried the estimate would become a self-fulfilling prophecy or, worse, that the U.S. had a hidden agenda for Nigeria. In Abuja, the U.S. ambassador met with the special committee to discuss the NIC report. He attempted to explain how the NIC operates and put its judgments in proper perspective. In addition, former Nigerian ambassador to the United States Jibrin Aminu, who chaired the Senate Foreign Relations Committee, flew to Washington to get a clearer idea of the report's significance. According to Nigerian senatorial participants, two phrases in the publicized report caused special offense: the idea that Nigeria would become a failed state and that it might collapse. There also was some worry about the reference to possible military coups.

That a U.S. government agency views Nigeria as a possible failed state has had a sobering impact on Nigerian leaders and entered public discourse at the same time that the NPRC was discussing the future of the political system in Nigeria. Hopefully, the Nigerian democratic process is vibrant enough to engage these challenges and projections of potential instability. But the U.S. report, whatever the realities involved, has overshadowed public discourse at all levels on the full range of scenarios for Nigeria, including how to get to best-case scenarios (which usually involve avoiding worst-case scenarios).

This monograph has argued that if the five challenges of nation building are met, Nigeria will have a bright future. Judging from the past, it seems highly likely that Nigeria will muddle through. Fortunately, a vibrant multi-party political system allows for opposition voices to speak hard truths and identify the problems for the Nigerian people—and at least to provide cautions to those in power.

The dominant voice of these opposition parties is Muhammadu Buhari, the ANPP candidate for president in 2003 and 2007. He had taken the lead in challenging the 2003 election results in the courts and in calling attention to underlying problems in society that require urgent attention. And he is widely recognized as a concerned Nigerian by the international community. In a 2004 speech in Washington, Buhari articulated some of the elements of the Vision 2010 worst-case scenario:

> An unstable Nigeria driven by internal wars, insurrections, or other manifestations of a failed state has the potential to destabilize the whole continent of Africa. The common symptomatic phenomena of internal disarray by way of civil wars and refugees and internally displaced persons have been dealt with by the world with varying successes in the past. But the break-up of Nigeria with a population of 130 million will produce a refugee crisis of unimaginable proportions. African countries will be overwhelmed and both Europe and Asia will be under severe strain. The highest number of refugees the world has had to deal with has never exceeded 25 million, with another 30 million or so displaced

persons. This is about one-third of the refugee potential of a war-
torn Nigeria. The international community, especially the U.S. will
see it in their interest to forestall this major tragedy for Africa and
the world.[6]

This nightmare scenario would emerge again the year after Buhari's presentation as Nigeria went through a wrenching period during which the
validity of a third term for the country's president dominated the political
landscape for six months between November 2005 and May 2006. The international community uniformly expressed concern over the sociopolitical implications of a third term for incumbents.[7]

Even Muhammadu Buhari outlined the dire consequences of a third term:

> No doubt, the year 2007 [when elections would be held] comes
> with great portends of danger. Even without the additional peril
> posed to the country by the deeply unpopular planned constitu-
> tional review to give the regime another term in office, we ought
> to have been concerned about the direction of events in Nigeria.
> The danger signals have been all too visible. After seven years
> of corruption, economic mismanagement and a general lacklus-
> ter performance by the new democratic dispensation in Nigeria,
> people's frustration and anger are at an all-time high. There is
> no doubt that a violent resistance will be unleashed throughout
> the country, especially if, as is widely feared, the government
> decides to ignore the sanction of the National Assembly. . . . But
> what is not known exactly is what nature the violent resistance
> will take. Left on its own, it is most unlikely that the uncoordi-
> nated response of the people to this will coalesce into popular
> mass action directed against the regime. There is the genuine
> fear that it may be hijacked by the government and diverted into
> either a communal crisis or religious riot in order to defeat the
> people. Within the last seven years several religious riots have
> erupted all over the country and many have seen evidence of
> the hands of government in almost all of time. . . . And concur-
> rently with the religious crises there had been a series of com-
> munal clashes—sometimes simultaneously and other times in
> rapid succession—and sometimes one as the fall-out of the other.
> In some of the cases [of violence] this was the direct result of
> Obasanjo's sustained efforts to polarize the country along ethnic
> lines and especially along the North-South divide. It is the well

---

6. Muhammadu Buhari, "Alternative Perspectives on Nigeria's Political Evolution,"
   speech given at Woodrow Wilson International Center for Scholars, Washington, D.C.,
   April 7, 2004.

7. See, for example, "In Nigeria, Things Fall Apart," *New York Times*, March 26, 2006, and Peter
   Lewis and Princeton Lyman, "Nigeria on the Edge," *Wall Street Journal*, April 3, 2006.

> known tactic of divide-and-rule playing on the fears of one side
> and employing it to defeat the other.[8]

Meanwhile, John Negroponte, U.S. director of national intelligence, had testified before Congress in February 2006 that if President Obasanjo stayed on beyond his two-term limit, he might "unleash major turmoil and conflict" leading to a "disruption of oil supply, secessionist moves by regional governments, major refugee flows, and instability elsewhere in west Africa." These remarks were widely circulated in Nigeria and sparked debate about the linkage between issues of term limits, democracy, and violence.

Additionally, the U.S. State Department released its Human Rights Report in early March 2006, accusing Nigeria of having a poor human rights record. Listed abuses included "abridgment of citizens' rights to change their government, politically motivated and extra-judicial killings by security forces and use of excessive force."

Political Turnover Prospects

With the Nigerian national census scheduled for March 21–26, 2006, and political tensions rising, the central issue was whether President Obasanjo would ignore or modify constitutional term limits and seek a third term after his second term expired in May 2007. The 1999 Constitution of the Federal Republic of Nigeria was clear, stating, "A person shall not be qualified for election to the office of President if . . . he has been elected to such office at any two previous elections."[9] Amendments were allowed, however, if "approved by the votes of not less than two-thirds majority of all the members of that House and approved by resolution of the Houses of Assembly of not less than two-thirds of all the states."[10] Enormous pressure was on legislators, governors, and others to support this third-term initiative. Yet, there was widespread resistance to the move, especially in the north. Lawyers and courts throughout the country observed a two-day strike in March. Even the Nigerian Roman Catholic bishops came out strongly opposing the third term.[11] The Arewa Consultative Forum (ACF)—the major northern elite sounding board—declared that it would not recognize an Obasanjo presidency after May 2007. (The chairman of the AFC, a northern Yoruba Christian, wrote a personal letter to Obasanjo asking him to pull back from the emerging third-term crisis.)

---

8. Muhammadu Buhari, "How Prepared Are We for Possible Upheaval in Nigeria?" (Forum 2007, Africans in America and Nigerian Social Workers Association, New York, April 29, 2006).

9. Constitution of the Federal Republic of Nigeria (1999), chapter 4, section 137.

10. Ibid., chapter 1, section 9.

11. "Bishops Urge Retention of Term Limits in Nigeria," *Washington Post*, March 13, 2006.

At a grassroots level, the political frustrations may have contributed to sectarian violence, including the so-called Prophet Muhammad cartoon riots, which left about 150 people dead, mainly in the northeastern states, followed by reprisals in the southeast. The national Muslim organizations and the Christian Association of Nigeria called for peace and characterized the riots as political rather than religious.

The official Nigerian National Commission for Refugees reported in March 2006 that three million people had been displaced and a minimum of fourteen thousand killed by ethnoreligious violence since the return to democratic rule in 1999.[12] The commission placed much of the blame for such violence on the legacy of military rule in Nigeria. Yet Nigeria's military legacy, which may well have contained most violence during the 1984–99 period, is hardly an explanation for the subsequent political turmoil.

The rejection of the third-term option by the Nigerian Senate in mid-May 2006 seemed to put an end to some of the political pressures contributing to turmoil, but the struggle for power was far from over. Some politicians feared that the president's "Plan B" might welcome violence, which would require a constitutionally sanctioned state of emergency and hence an extension of his term. Even voices from the southwest, such as the Pan-Yoruba sociopolitical organization, Afenifere, cautioned against civil war as a result of Obasanjo's third-term agenda.[13] How then did Nigerian political elites step back from the brink and move forward into a power shift to the north in 2007?

Power Sharing and Power Shifting in the 2007 Election

This section addresses six aspects of regional and Muslim-Christian political balancing in Nigeria, as illuminated by the 2007 election: assessing the 2007 presidential election; the religious balance factor in Nigerian politics; Fourth Republic power sharing and power shifting; postelection reactions; the legitimating role of traditional emirs and chiefs in northern Nigeria; and the challenges ahead.

Assessing the 2007 Presidential Election

The 2007 presidential election was seen as a bellwether event in ethnoreligious power sharing, because the three major parties enabled the shift in power from a southern Christian presidential candidate to a northern Muslim candidate.

---

12. "Violence Left 3 Million Bereft in past 7 Years," *New York Times*, March 14, 2006. The article notes, "The hardest hit area has been the oil-producing Niger Delta region, in the south. The commission said 700,000 had been driven from their homes in Delta State in 2003 by ethnic fighting over control of Warri city and by conflicts involving militias."
13. See "Don't Cause Civil War, Afenifere Tells Obasanjo," *ThisDay*, April 27, 2006.

In December 2006 the dominant political party, the PDP, held its nomination convention. The incumbent president, Obasanjo, had not tipped his hand in terms of a successor. The obvious pool of candidates from both north and south included various individuals from the private and public sectors as well as former state governors (most of whom were subject to term limits as governors) and retired military generals (many of whom had previous experience in national leadership positions).

The major PDP northern governors in contention were Ibrahim Saminu Turaki (Jigawa), having crossed the carpet from his earlier ANPP affiliation, Ahmed Makarfi (Kaduna), Umaru Musa Yar'Adua (Katsina), and Abdullahi Adamu (Nasarawa). Former northern senior military or security officers included Aliyu Gusau (Zamfara, immediate past national security adviser), Mohammed Buba Marwa (Adamawa, former military governor of Borno and Lagos states), Ibrahim Babangida (Niger, former military head of state), and Mamman Kontagora (Niger, former minister of works and housing).

The most obvious omission from this PDP list was the incumbent vice president, Atiku Abubakar (Adamawa), who had launched his presidential campaign in Abuja on November 25.[14] He had become disenchanted with the PDP and was in the process of setting up a new party, the Action Congress, with many of his PDP colleagues. His campaign launch in November was attended by most of the former Alliance for Democracy (AD) governors from the southwest states.

At the same time, many southern candidates in the PDP presented themselves to the nominating convention in hopes that a power-shift agreement with the north would not hold. The southern PDP governors who were candidates included Sam Egwu (Ebonyi), Chimaroke Nnamani (Enugu), Achike Udenwa (Imo), Victor Attah (Akwa-Ibom), David Duke (Cross-River), and Peter Odili (Rivers). Former military officers included Ebitu Ukiwe (Abia, second in command to General Babangida) and Mike Okhai Akhigbe (Edo, second in command to General Abdulsalami). In a surprise move, President Obasanjo managed to get most of the above to withdraw in favor of his own presidential candidate, Umaru Yar'Adua, along with his vice-presidential choice, Jonathan Goodluck, governor of Bayelsa State in the south-south.

Within the ANPP, whose convention followed that of the PDP, the two major announced candidates were Ahmed Sani (Zamfara) and Muhammadu Buhari (Katsina). The latter was former head of state (1984–85) and ANPP candidate in 2003 and had served as unofficial leader of the opposition over the past several years. In an interesting maneuver, Governor Sani (who goes by his traditional title, *yerima*) had arranged for many of his followers to be del-

---

14. See speech by Atiku Abubakar, GCON, on the occasion of his declaration for the presidency of Nigeria in the 2007 election, at the old parade ground, area 10, Garki, Abuja, Amanaonline, December 1, 2006.

egates to the ANPP convention. At the last minute, however, Sani withdrew, and the nomination went to Buhari.

The other two significant northern-based parties also selected their candidates. The Action Congress selected Vice President Atiku Abubakar, and the Democratic Peoples Party selected Attahiru Bafarawa, governor of Sokoto.

By January 2007 it was clear that there would be a power shift from a southern president to a northern president. The obvious question was how to persuade the southern states to accept this course. Incumbency was not an issue because of the two-term limits on incumbents. The question would come down to party organization and discipline, funding, cross-regional linkages, and whether the PDP government would play by the legal and constitutional rules in running the election. Would the Independent National Electoral Commission (INEC) be prepared for the election? Would the police and security agencies be neutral? Would the PDP access to enormous financial resources corrupt the process? With twenty-five presidential contenders representing a range of parties, could there be a possible runoff if no one received the necessary distribution requirements on the first ballot?

Unfortunately, the international observers of the April 2007 presidential election felt it was deeply flawed. The International Republican Institute (IRI) declared it was the worst election they had ever seen. The European Union delegation regarded it as a "charade" and did not accept the results. A partial exception was ECOWAS, which receives much of its financing from Nigeria and put a somewhat positive face on the election in the "glass is half full" tradition. Nigerian domestic observers, however, were adamant that the election was flawed and should be rerun.

The U.S. National Democratic Institute (NDI), which had sent a team to observe the election, issued a statement on April 23, 2007, stating:

> In many places, and in a number of ways, the electoral process failed the Nigerian people. . . . A major problem that marred this stage of the electoral process was that polling stations in many states opened hours late, closed early or failed to open at all. . . . delegates were disheartened by the relatively low voter turnout, which both voters and polling officials attributed to problems, including violence, experienced during and after the April 14th state elections. The serious flaws witnessed during this electoral process threaten to further erode citizen confidence in the country's democratic institutions. . . . The delegation believes that the expeditious adjudication and resolution of legal complaints arising from the polls is a vital component of this process. . . . On a positive note, on April 21st the delegation observed a relatively smooth electoral process in some parts of the Federal Capital Territory, Niger, Plateau and Lagos states. . . . However, in the preponderance of places the delegates visited, such as Abia, Adamawa, Anambra, Bauchi, Benue, Cross River,

Enugu, Kaduna, Katsina, Ogun and Oyo states, a different picture emerged.

The NDI statement went on to list specific irregularities, including

- balloting material delays, preventing polls from opening on time or at all;
- inadequate supplies of many voting items, especially ballots for both presidential and legislative elections;
- improperly prepared balloting materials for legislative elections, which did not include all candidates;
- inadequate facilities for voting;
- lack of privacy when voting;
- vote counting process that made it vulnerable to manipulation and difficult to verify votes;
- poor registration of voters and techniques to identify voters, and inadequate polling stations leading to crowded conditions.

The NDI also reported that while preelection violence decreased before the April 21 polling, it was troubled that political parties used youths as protective wings before and on election day. Security agents also were reported to have stuffed ballot boxes, and stories of intimidation by party agents and vote buying abounded. "In all places, ballot security was severely compromised as a result of the presidential ballot lacking serial numbers. This makes the system susceptible to abuse and will make it impossible to verify the accuracy of the results."[15]

When asked by Nigerian reporters at the NDI press conference in Abuja on April 23 what grade she would give to the election, the chairman of the NDI Board of Directors and former U.S. secretary of state Madeleine Albright replied that as a university professor she was a tough grader and would assign the process an F. She also called for the head of the Independent National Election Commission (INEC) to be fired.

The Presidential Election in Katsina State, April 2007: Author's Observations

The case of Katsina State in the far north illustrates some of these problems. It was also the home state of the two top presidential candidates, Umaru

---

15. The full text of the NDI statement on the April 21 election is available on the NDI Web site, http://ndi.org. A compilation of various international and domestic observer reports was published in Nigeria after the elections by Nigerians United for Democracy, *Mirror of a Fraudulent Election* (May 2007). For a harsh critique in the international media by a knowledgeable observer, see Jean Herskovits, "Nigeria's Rigged Democracy," *Foreign Affairs* 86, no. 4, (July–August 2007), 115–30.

Yar'Adua of the PDP and governor of Katsina State and Muhammadu Buhari of the ANPP, originally from Daura in the far north of the state. The NDI international observation team in Katsina was made up of two individuals representing NGOs and academia: Pauline Baker, president of Fund for Peace, and myself. We were joined by Halima Ben Umar, national director of Women in Media in Nigeria, who is originally from Kano and represented Nigerian domestic observers. Baker digitally photographed virtually all aspects of our observation of the Katsina election during the polling center phase, including instances of flagrant abuse.[16]

On election day, we stayed mainly in the Katsina urban area and surrounding villages. Security concerns were paramount. We were unable to visit Daura where the election office was burned down by angry voters after an insufficient number of ballots was made available in the morning. When the polls closed at five o'clock, we were also advised by security personnel not to observe the collation process since mobs of disgruntled youth were milling around the collation centers. We were further advised by security to leave by six o'clock on the morning after the election due to fears of violence after results were announced. (European Union observers told us that the violent disturbances in Katsina a week earlier had started in our hotel.) On our eight-hour drive back to Abuja from Katsina, we had to avoid burning tires in the middle of the road in the town of Malamfashi as anger and frustration mounted.

Throughout election day, however, we were able to observe twenty polling stations selected at random in the Katsina urban area and surrounding rural areas and to speak with numerous people in both Hausa and English. We recorded concerns expressed by voters about what was going on. Of paramount concern was the lack of serial numbers on the presidential ballots, making it easy to add fraudulent votes as votes were counted. When we pointed this out to a polling agent, he replied, "This is the Nigerian factor."

We also noticed large numbers of underage youths voting and were told the going rate per vote was N1,000, although the voter was left with only N400 after middle parties had taken their share. At one polling station, we actually observed a woman sitting at a small table near the polling area, handing out N1,000 notes to prospective voters. We were told she was acting on behalf of the PDP. At another location, we saw a man with a PDP shirt handing out money to young boys to vote at a nearby polling station. Since we were committed to observing and not interfering with the election process, we were unable to confront such abuses directly.

Having observed previous elections, we were struck by the low turnout throughout the day. However, at one polling station closing at 4:20 p.m. we asked how many people had voted and were told 1,700. We asked to see the

---

16. These photos from Katsina are freely available in a photo essay on the Fund for Peace Web site, http://fundforpeace.org.

ballot box, which was in a back room. It was clear from visual inspection that the transparent box was only about one-quarter full, with perhaps 125 ballots. At another polling station at around 4:30 p.m. the police came and took away the ballot boxes "to protect them," even though there were still voters in line.

Upon returning from Katsina to Abuja the day after the election, we were asked to submit both summary and detailed reports to the full delegation on what we observed at the Katsina polling stations. The summary coding for the twenty stations is listed in table 3.

Our strong impression in Katsina was that the incumbent party had a clear advantage over opposition groups due to control of the election machinery, the police, and financial resources. Without access to specific polling center results, it is hard to assess whether or to what extent results were manipulated. We were aware that both Yar'Adua and Buhari were popular candidates in Katsina State, but the electoral machinery makes it difficult or impossible to judge if the announced results were legitimate. The actual numbers were not released down to the level of the polling station.

The Religious Balance Factor in Nigerian Politics

Despite the flaws of the presidential election, this election was significant because it sought to balance the interests and identities of the two major regions in the country: north and south. All major parties accepted this basic political necessity.

Although religious identity is closely related to issues of ethnic and regional identity, religious identity issues are especially sensitive. As noted previously, this is an area where Nigerians have devised a number of socioeconomic and political mechanisms to manage potential conflict and encourage cooperation and indeed to use surrogate identities to mitigate this issue, as summarized in table 4.

The presidential election of 2007 and its aftermath cannot be understood outside the Fourth Republic and its attempts to create religious balance throughout the country's institutions. As noted previously, a long history is behind this approach, beginning with the country's colonial legacy of treating northern and southern Nigeria as separate entities; the use of indirect rule, especially in the north, which empowered the preexisting emirate system and solidified the legacy of sharia law; the breakdown of the First Republic in 1966 and the civil war (1967–70); the various military coups and countercoups; and the changing external environment and rise of an oil-driven economy.

Fourth Republic Power Sharing and Power Shifting

Promulgated in May 1999, the Fourth Republic constitution was based on the 1979 constitution (a presidential/federal model) and hence the rules were reasonably well known. To ensure a national base, a presidential candidate

TABLE 3. INCIDENT REPORTS OF TWENTY POLLING STATIONS, APRIL 2007

Incident	Number out of Twenty Polling Places
Disenfranchisement due to early closing	20
Insufficient voting materials	18
Insufficient polling officials	0
Secrecy of ballot compromised	20
Chaos in polling station	10
Polling stations never opened	3
Violence on election day[a]	0
Intimidation, harassment, bribery	10
Improper conduct by security agents	1
Limiting rights of observers and party agents	0
Ballot box stealing or missing	5
Underage voting	10

a. There were expressions of fear of violence, however, and some polling agents
    called for more security before allowing the ballots to be counted.

had to achieve 25 percent of the votes in two-thirds of the states to win. If no
candidate achieved this goal, a runoff election would be held between the
two top contenders.

In 1999, the PDP, with its balanced ticket of President Olusegun Obasanjo (a
born-again Christian from Ogun state in the southwest) and Atiku Abubakar
(a northern Muslim from Adamawa state in the northeast) appeared to prevail
with about 62 percent of the vote. The major opposition party—the All People's
Party (APP)—also nominated its presidential candidate from the southwest
(Olu Falae) and its vice-presidential candidate from the Muslim north (Umaru
Shinkafi). This was seen as a concession to the need for a power shift to the
Christian southwest after years of northern Muslim military rule. In addition,
there was need to assuage the angry southwest after the imprisonment and
death of a Yoruba Muslim, M. K. O. Abiola, who was judged by most to have
won the 1993 election. The military regime of Sani Abacha had thrown Abiola
into prison where he died.

The election in 1999 also seemed to suffer, with violence and allegations
of fraud and intimidation in many parts of the country. Yet it appears that
a gentleman's agreement was established among several factions within the
PDP and that after two terms the next presidential candidate would hail from
the Muslim north and the vice president from the Christian south.

The subsequent election in April 2003 saw two major political parties in
contention: the PDP and the ANPP, heir to the APP. The incumbents in the
PDP faced off against Muhammadu Buhari (a northern Muslim from Kat-

TABLE 4. MANAGING ETHNORELIGIOUS DIVERSITY IN NIGERIA

Issue	Mechanism to Avoid Conflict
Designing and reporting population census	Questions of religious or ethnic identity are not asked.
Achieving political-party balance on national tickets	Widespread agreement among the major parties that a presidential candidate who is a northern Muslim should have a vice-presidential candidate who is a southern Christian, and vice versa, recognizing the widely accepted notion of power sharing.
Handling of ethnoreligious labeling of political parties	Such labeling is not acceptable.
Implementing the principle of north-south power shifting	After a presidential term or two by a person from a Christian/southern region, the rotation shifts to a person of a Muslim/northern regional zone, and vice versa.
Lessening the impact of religious and ethnic identities to encourage cohesion	North-south regionalism is strong, but six geopolitical zones, divided equally between northern and southern Nigeria, are used as surrogates to blur ethnoreligious distinctions.
Encouraging the federal character principle in the constitution through power sharing at the federal executive level, including the cabinet	One minister from each of the thirty-six states is appointed to the cabinet.
Covering issues such as sharia law and religious conflict by the media	While there is extensive press freedom, most serious newspapers, the electronic media, and other outlets are aware of the need not to be alarmist.
Establishing the symbolism of a "nonpreferentialist" religious balance at the national level	The federal capital has been located close to the center of the country with a national mosque and a Christian ecumenical center.
Encouraging residential housing patterns in metropolitan centers to reduce conflict	From colonial times, most cities have established "new city" areas for migrants from other zones or regions.
Sharing the national budget—largely funded by oil revenues—in a transparent and balanced way among the states	Derivation principles require "revenue sharing" based on constitutional principles of population, levels of development, and origins of petroleum resources.
Dealing with interfaith conflict	Interfaith conflict mediation centers are encouraged at all levels, especially in ethnoreligious "mixed" areas, such as Kaduna or Jos, and at the national level in Abuja.
Promoting interfaith communication and cooperation	The Nigeria Inter-Religious Council (NIREC), consisting of twenty-five Muslim leaders and twenty-five Christian leaders, and cochaired by the Sultan of Sokoto (as President of NSCIA) and the president of CAN, meet regularly to enhance interfaith communication and cooperation.
Linking disparate groups in many other areas of daily life and business organization	Business organizations often intentionally select partners from cross-regional or interfaith pools.

sina state) and Chuba Okadigbo (southeastern Christian) of the ANPP. Again, the PDP claimed to win with about 62 percent of the popular vote and met the 25 percent, two-thirds distribution requirement. The incumbency factor seemed to prevail, but with the expectation that the constitutional two-term limit would mean a power shift in the April 2007 elections. Again, allegations of rigging and fraud were rampant, but the opposition parties, led by Buhari, took the matter to the courts. In July 2005 the Supreme Court decided in favor of the PDP, and Buhari, as de facto leader of the opposition, accepted the results, although he still contended that the election was rigged.

After an anxious period during the first half of 2006, when the president tried to change the constitution to allow for a third term, the major parties held primaries and conventions to select candidates. Because of a split within the PDP between the president and vice president, a new party was created, the Action Congress, which nominated Atiku Abubakar for president and Ben Obi (from the southeast) for vice president. Meanwhile, President Obasanjo and the PDP made every effort to keep Atiku Abubakar off the ballot on grounds of corruption. The matter was finally resolved five days before the April 2007 election when the Supreme Court ruled in favor of Atiku.

As noted earlier, the PDP nominated as its presidential candidate the governor of Katsina State in the far north. Umaru Musa Yar'Adua was from a distinguished family. His father was a minister in the First Republic and an emirate title holder in Katsina (*tafida*). His elder brother (Shehu Musa) was a major presidential candidate in the aborted Third Republic.[17] Umaru holds the emirate title of *mutawalli*, but apart from his two terms as governor, he was really not involved in politics. His major advantages were that he was seen as noncorrupt and that he was the heir to his brother's political machine. Furthermore, the Yar'Adua family was extremely close to President Obasanjo and could be trusted with his legacy. On the negative side, Yar'Adua had health problems and was not very charismatic.[18] Even his campaign posters in Katsina used the slogan, "The Silent Achiever."[19] The PDP vice-presidential candidate was the governor of Bayelsa State in the oil-producing south-south. Goodluck Jonathan clearly balanced the ticket in terms of Muslim-Christian and north-south identities and had the added advantage of being from

---

17. See Shehu Musa Yar'Adua Foundation, *Shehu Musa Yar'Adua: A Life of Service* (Abuja, 2004). Note: this book makes numerous references to Shehu's junior brother, Umaru Yar'Adua, including his work managing Sambo farms.

18. Umaru Yar'Adua requires kidney dialysis on a regular basis.

19. In 2007, Umaru Musa Yar'Adua was fifty-six years old. He attended Government College, Keffi, and Ahmadu Bello University, Zaria, earning a master's degree in chemistry with a focus on analytical chemistry. In 1976 he began his career as a lecturer at Katsina College of Arts, Science and Technology. He moved to Katsina Polytechnic in 1979. He was a member of the People's Redemption Party (PRP) under Mallam Aminu Kano and was secretary of the People's Front of Nigeria (PFN), the precursor of the PDP.

the Ijaw ethnic area, where much of the oil-fields insurgency was based.[20] It was thought that he could "fix" the problem of insurgency in the Delta. The ANPP again selected Muhammadu Buhari as its presidential candidate. The vice-presidential candidate was Edwin Ume-Ezeoke, a former speaker of the House of Representatives and national chairman of the ANPP from the Christian southeast zone. Thus, all three of the major candidates in the April 2007 presidential election—representing the PDP, ANPP, and AC, respectively—were northern Muslims with southern Christians as running mates. Clearly, there would be a power shift from the south to the north. In all, there were twenty-five presidential candidates on the ballot, with most representing state-level "favorite sons."

Preelection polling in Nigeria during January and February 2007 actually put Buhari well ahead of Yar'Adua in the north. There was speculation that the ANPP and AC would create an alliance to challenge the PDP, especially in the southwest and southeast. A broader question was whether the range of opposition candidates could cooperate in some way to check the incumbent PDP. Clearly, this might have happened if a runoff election were possible.

In the end, the INEC, despite promises to run an efficient and fair election, simply made a mess of the April 14 gubernatorial and state-level elections. The last-minute addition of Atiku Abubakar's name to the presidential list—after the state-level elections, which, with a few exceptions, were swept by the PDP—created further confusion. During this brief interlude (April 14–21), the time seemed right for the opposition parties to cooperate and confront the PDP.

The question in many minds was whether the INEC's failure on April 14 was based on incompetence or intention. The opposition parties met in Abuja during the week between April 14 and the scheduled April 21 elections and initially decided to boycott the April 21 election on grounds that it would be rigged by the INEC and that there was no time to correct the obvious mistakes. At the last minute, Buhari prevailed and insisted that in order to challenge the outcome of the elections in the courts, the parties had to contest. But the boycott agreement broke down, and confusion reigned.

The killing of a prominent cleric, Shaykh Ja'afaru Adam, in Kano just before the April 21 election and the subsequent murder of police in Kano by the so-called Taliban created a sense of insecurity and apprehension, and international observers were not sent to Kano. There was a parallel crisis in

---

20. In 2007, Goodluck Ebele Jonathan was fifty years old. He holds a bachelor's degree in zoology, a master's in hydrobiology/fisheries (in biology), and a doctorate in zoology from the University of Port Harcourt. He began teaching in secondary school and later lectured at Rivers State College of Science and Technology, now Rivers State University of Science and Technology. He then transferred to the Oil Minerals Producing Areas Development Commission as head of the fisheries department. He resigned in 1998 and in 1999 became deputy to Governor Alamieyeseigha. He became governor of Bayelsa on December 12, 2005, after Alamieyeseigha's impeachment.

Port Harcourt (Rivers State), during which a number of police stations were burned after insurgents stole the AK-47s that had been ordered to reinforce the police during the elections. Again, most observers avoided this area.

As noted, the presidential election of April 21 was judged by the international and domestic observers to have been a failure or a charade or both. The official results were announced by the INEC chair, Maurice Iwu, on Monday, April 23: Yar'Adua had received 24-plus million votes, Buhari, 6-plus million votes, and Atiku Abubakar 2-plus million votes, for a total of about 32 million votes out of a total registration of 61 million. This 72 percent landslide for the PDP, along with the more than 50 percent voter turnout, was simply not credible to most observers.

Postelection Reactions

Opposition leaders along with civil society groups and the Nigerian Labor Congress called for demonstrations on May 1 (May Day). Yet the inspector general of police did not issue permits for these political demonstrations and instead ordered his men to use maximum force (widely interpreted as shoot to kill) to prevent demonstrations. Civil-society leaders were arrested, while still insisting the elections be canceled within fourteen days. Labor and civil-society groups called a national protest strike for May 29. (This strike was most noticeable in Kano and Lagos, although many in Abuja stayed home in protest as well.)

The international community took a cautious wait-and-see approach as events unfolded, realizing that with the inauguration ceremony scheduled for May 29, the de facto government of Umaru Yar'Adua and the PDP would need to be recognized.[21] At the same time, members of the international community called for election issues to be taken to the election tribunals, that is, courts set up to adjudicate election complaints, and not to the streets. Meanwhile, domestic groups claimed that election tribunals were creatures of the PDP and ineffective. The spotlight clearly focused on the independence and integrity of the judicial system.[22]

Encouraging news began to emerge as the tribunals undertook their work. On October 10, 2007, an election tribunal called for fresh elections in Kogi

---

21. The United States was represented at the inauguration by Assistant Secretary of State Jendayi Frazer. Since many other countries were represented by heads of state or more senior officials, this was intended to send a message that the United States was not happy with the election process.

22. Buhari and the ANPP went to court to petition for the annulment of the presidential election and for a new election on grounds that ballots were not available at the polling stations. The Atiku Abubakar organization also insisted through the courts that the presidential election be rerun. In late May 2007, the courts upheld the right of the plaintiffs to access INEC data on which the results were premised. The head of INEC, however, refused to turn over such information, at least until after the inauguration. Subsequently, the ANPP withdrew its court appeal after two ministries were awarded to ANPP stalwarts. However, Buhari persisted in his appeal.

State. Also, fresh elections were set for Kebbi State. In Rivers State there had been a reversal of the election results. By November 2007, it was expected that the election tribunals would complete their work by February 2008.

Meanwhile, a high-level election reform commission, established by President Yar'Adua and headed by former chief justice Muhammad Lawal Uwais, began a serious inquiry into the problems of the electoral system. The commission gathered evidence in fall 2007 and expected to schedule public hearings throughout the country starting in February 2008 once the election tribunals had completed their work. The commission expected to make its final report public in August 2008.

While the presidential election of April 2007 was seriously flawed (or even nonexistent in about fifteen of the thirty-six states), the big picture was clear. With twenty-nine of thirty-six state governors and about 72 percent of the presidential vote in the PDP camp, Nigeria seemed to be sliding toward a single-party system, enforced by a dominant incumbent party, while at the same time allowing for a power shift from south to north.

Fortunately, the protests after the April elections have not taken on a religious tone. That the major opposition party candidates were from the north and civil-society groups of all descriptions condemned the elections meant that Muslim-Christian identity politics were taken off the front burner. Thus, the Nigerian Supreme Council for Islamic Affairs (NSCIA), through its secretary-general, Lateef Adegbite, along with many other Muslim groups observing the elections, were in league with their Christian colleagues—not to mention such mixed groups as the Nigerian Bar Association (NBA)—in condemning the elections. This has created a sense of "in-group/out-group" politics not based on religious identity, which many see as a positive sign.

The PDP attempted to achieve legitimacy after the election. At the national level, considerable pressure was applied to the royal fathers—traditional rulers—throughout the country to get behind the new government. Yar'Adua traveled around Africa to secure recognition as the president-elect. Ironically, Yar'Adua has always been well regarded and may well have been successful even without the election rigging. Among other activities to influence the broader international community, professional lobbying organizations were hired. Domestic discontent was channeled through election tribunals, and preparations were made for a major inauguration ceremony, which would include foreign leaders, key elements of domestic constituencies, and the Nigerian royal fathers.[23] The inauguration was especially vital as it would confer legitimacy to the new government. Indeed, in traditional northern

---

23. Opposition parties used some of these same tactics in reverse to delegitimize the government, especially travels abroad, lobbying, and use of the media.

culture, it is this public indication of support that is most essential. How, then, does this traditional aspect of legitimacy work in practice?

The Legitimating Role of Traditional Emirs and Chiefs in Northern Nigeria

As during the military periods, a key linkage between the federal government in Abuja and the people at the grassroots level has been the institution of the traditional royal fathers, such as emirs and chiefs, who were accepted as legitimate local leaders. For the most part, if these personages accepted the federal government, so did the citizens. This was particularly true in the north, where the authority of the emirs and chiefs was probably enhanced during the colonial period. Even though their real powers to govern were stripped during the independence era, in the eyes of their followers, their legitimacy and influence have persisted. The federal government can, however, depose these local rulers, including the sultans. Hence, there are checks and balances even for traditional rulers.

This returns us to the significance of another major succession event of 2006–07, the selection of a new sultan of Sokoto, who is the formal head of Nigeria's 70 million Muslims. The sultan of Sokoto, Alhaji Muhammad Sa'ad Abubakar, was elected by the kingmaker council of Sokoto, a kind of electoral college, on November 2, 2006, after the death of the incumbent, his elder brother. Sa'ad Abubakar's name had been submitted to this special council at the last minute by the governor to be considered with other candidates. No doubt there would have been disappointed contenders after the election, but the installation process was meant to reconcile such factions. At the formal ceremony on March 3, 2007, in Sokoto attended by President Obasanjo—even Vice President Atiku Abubakar made a surprise visit—the international community was widely represented. The heads of various districts, key extended-family members in Sokoto, and other royal fathers from throughout the country were also present. In short, the public support and respect shown by the wider community confirmed the legitimacy of the election.

It was this type of inauguration that outgoing president Obasanjo and the PDP hoped to emulate to give legitimacy to the presidential elections on the national level. According to Nigerian press reports, the enormous sum of N32 billion (about $250 million) was marked for the May 29 inauguration.[24] As things turned out, most royal fathers stayed in their home states because of the gubernatorial installations held at the time of the national inauguration. The sultan did come to Abuja for the installation but kept a low profile. How-

---

24. Spokesmen for the newly elected president claim the cost figure for the inauguration was much lower. Obviously, it depends on which costs are included. For instance, more than fifty thousand police were deployed in Abuja for the inauguration.

ever, once the Chief Justice swore in the new president on May 29, the constitutional mandate was clear, and the sultan recognized President Yar'Adua as
legitimate. In mid-June he made a courtesy call on President Yar'Adua, along
with a delegation of the NSCIA.[25] It remains to be seen whether the flawed
election process can be overcome through the legitimation process of the
installation on May 29.[26] Many key personalities, including the sultan and
Yar'Adua himself, have said they will follow whatever decisions are made by
the Supreme Court regarding the election.

How the international community reacted at the time of his inauguration also became a crucial message, even though de facto recognition is a
diplomatic art and does not confer the same degree of "legitimacy" as de
jure recognition. Disappointed candidate and outgoing vice president Atiku
Abubakar chose not to confer recognition of the new president but to remain
in the United States during the inauguration for "health reasons."[27] In terms
of "popular" response, as noted earlier, there was a national strike called for
May 29, although it occurred mainly in Kano and Lagos. It appeared that
many Nigerians at the grassroots level were simply too intimidated, discour-
aged, or preoccupied to worry about "legitimation" of the new administration one way or the other.

The Challenges Ahead

While much of the focus in Nigeria after May 29, 2007, has been on the
flawed elections of April 2007, the larger picture should be on the power-

---

25. See "NSCIA Declares Support for New Govt," *Daily Trust*, June 19, 2007, which reported
"The Sultan of Sokoto, Alhaji Sa'ad Abubakar III, yesterday threw his weight behind the
administration of President Umaru Yar'Adua, charging him to ensure fairness, equity, and
justice in his dealings with all sections of the country.... The royal father advised president
Yar'Adua to always remember the admonition of the legendary Sheik Uthman ben Fodio,
which states: 'A leader gains victory over his adversaries according to his justice over the
people, and is defeated in his struggles according to his injustice' .... Responding, President Yar'Adua thanked the NSCIA delegation and pledged to run a transparent and God
fearing government."

Members of the Sultan's delegation included the Shehu of Borno, Alhaji Umar Mustafa El-
Kanemi, representatives of the Emir of Kano, Alhaji Ado Bayero, Etsu Nupe, and Alhaji
Yahaya Abubakar, plus the Emir of Kazaure, the Emir of Birnin Gwari, the Emir of Suleja,
the NSCIA secretary (Abdul Lateef Adegbite), Sheikh Dahiru Bauchi, the Aare Musulumi of Yorubaland (Alhaji Arisekola Alao), the secretary-general of Jama'atu Nasril Islam,
Justice Abdul Qadri Orire, Sheikh Ahmad Lemu, the chief imam of the Abuja national
mosque, former deputy governor Alhajia Lateefah Okunnu, Group Captain Usman Jibrin,
and many others.

26. It will be some time before the actual pattern and attitude of traditional royal fathers at the
inauguration can be assessed, since outward appearances may be deceptive. The sultan
was caught in cross-pressures, since former governor of Sokoto, Attahiru Bafarawa, had
appointed him initially but then was defeated by the PDP at all levels in the messy April
election. Yet the sultan would be aware of his need to provide continuity within the ummah and at the national level during the political transition.

27. There is a long tradition in the north for disappointed candidates to leave the scene unless
willing to show symbolic obedience to the new ruler. Historically, a "flight" (*hijra*) was to
the east, en route to the holy lands in Arabia, thus taking on a religious tone.

sharing and power-shifting issues that are essential to Nigerian national unity. The 2007 elections represented a political crisis, but could they lead to religious sectarian violence?

While the northern Muslim community is divided among the three or more major political parties, southern-based parties or groups could become disillusioned to the point that localized secession movements (in the southeast or south-south, or even potentially in the southwest) begin to play on latent antinorthern, anti-Muslim sentiment. The question remains whether political mechanisms of power sharing, which have developed over the decades since independence, will be sufficient to strengthen and sustain national unity under such circumstances.

Nigeria has every chance to provide a model of Muslim-Christian cooperation based on the necessity for tolerance among people of the book (*ahl al-kitab*) and the obvious shared interests of its peoples. Whether the country can fulfill this promise will have consequences throughout Africa and beyond. The presidential election and inauguration of 2007 were intended to be a benchmark in this process of harmonious interfaith relations.

Meanwhile, the 2007 elections could have debilitating effects in all six geocultural zones. At the grassroots level, there is emerging a pervasive feeling of helplessness that powerful elites can manipulate their way to the top without meaningful change at the bottom and that political institutions have been degraded by years of corruption. In northern Nigeria, it was a similar failing of state institutions and lawlessness that led to the establishment of sharia law after 1999.

It is not clear whether Yar'Adua's presidency, or any actions his government might take to correct the abuses of the recent election, will reverse this palpable frustration of ordinary people. The 2007 election was a lost opportunity that could have made a mark in reversing the trend toward state decay. The policy of maximum force by the police to suppress discontent is an indication that the goal of a peaceful and democratic Nigeria has not yet been achieved.

Despite this bleak assessment, some senior northern Nigerian "notables" see three positive developments in the postelection period: a successful power shift to the north; voices of moderation encouraging people not to take to the streets; and a general consensus that the military is not an option. Another encouraging development is that for the first time in Nigerian history a university graduate has become head of state—not to mention that the vice president holds a science Ph.D. This sends a clear message that education, especially science education, is important. Northern Nigerian observers have noticed a far more "rational" tone in government with the new administration. In general, the tribunals, plus the election reform commission, are seen as credible.

Much work remains to establish the new federal government's domestic legitimacy. President Yar'Adua seems to be reaching out to his opponents and other key notables.[28] He will need to be seen as an independent actor rather than a puppet of Obasanjo.[29] Those who know him well insist that he is capable of this challenge. The "silent achiever," who in eight years as governor never visited the United States and is certainly not well known in Nigeria, will need to move quickly to consolidate a national government that is capable of meeting domestic and international challenges.[30]

Pathways of Political Change

In a nation as complex and diverse as Nigeria, there are usually three approaches to nation building, particularly among former colonial territories: partition the country into component parts; use force or the threat of force to hold the country's unlikely components together; or devise mechanisms of democratic federalism suitable to the demographic and political realities at hand. The basic question is always whether and how the goal of national unity can be achieved. The attempted partition by Biafra during the civil war (1967–70) is a stark reminder of the realities of the first possible approach and the high cost of failing to realize a workable political system. Military rule, including outright dictatorship with its extreme forms of centralization, is the second possible approach to the challenge of "keeping Nigeria one." Since many former military generals later may serve as civilian politicians, the tendency to overcentralization may also take civilian forms.

Democratic federalism, the third possible approach and the main focus of this monograph, must balance religious, ethnic, regional, economic, and political interests. As Nigeria moves through the twenty-first century, it must choose one of these three pathways of change—partition, centralization, or federalism.

---

28. President Yar'Adua's first appointment was Ambassador Baba Gana Kingibe, of Borno, to become secretary to the government, a key post. Kingibe had been M. K. O. Abiola's running mate in the 1992–93 elections on the Social Democratic Party (SDP) ticket. He served as foreign minister of Nigeria after 1993 and also minister of internal affairs and minister of power and steel. More recently, he was Nigeria's special envoy to Darfur in Sudan.

29. Yar'Adua's seven-point program is to focus on problems of power supply, inadequate infrastructure, education, agriculture, the Niger-Delta, unemployment, and other issues. Also, the PDP platform set "Vision 2020" goals, including making Nigeria one of the twenty strongest economies in the world by 2020.

30. Yar'Adua's visit to the United States in September 2007, as part of his appearance at the United Nations, was well received. When asked about the 2007 elections, he commented to the effect that no election is perfect. In mid-December 2007, Yar'Adua visited the White House after the meeting of the EU/AU summit in Lisbon.

Partition and Centralization

Apart from the occasional small ultrareligious communities in the far north, the main sentiment for partition comes from the southeast and south-south. Notably, these areas are overwhelmingly Christian with a mix of traditional or ethnic religions. They are also close to the sources of crude oil and gas.

In the Igbo-speaking southeast, the perceived exclusion from a major political role since the civil war has led to renewed nostalgia for an independent Biafra in some quarters. The organizational form of this sentiment comes from a movement known as the Movement for the Actualization of the Sovereign State of Biafra (MASSOB). Small groups of Nigerian expatriates from the southeast who are living abroad also share some of these hopes and visions. Memories of the history and horrors of the civil war also include the lack of reintegration of senior military officers after that conflict, although most other sectors of the southeast have been reincorporated. The occasional sectarian violence in the north since 1999 has sent alarms through the Igbo-Christian community, often resulting in reprisals against the small Hausa-Muslim communities living in the southeast. There may also be those in MASSOB who relish the idea of reinstating claims to some of the oil-producing areas in the south-south.

The Biafrian pound currency, although unofficial and "underground," is printed and circulated by the information and propaganda bureau of MASSOB. It is used as a medium of exchange in Benin and Cameroon, as well as in southern Nigeria. It is handled by Hausa currency traders throughout the country and, as of 2007, seemed to be appreciating against the U.S. dollar! It is not clear what the implications of this separatist currency phenomenon may turn out to be.

The political turmoil and sentiments for partition in the Niger Delta in the south-south is by far the most serious political development as of 2007. The Movement for the Emancipation of the Niger Delta (MEND) has been involved in armed insurgency, kidnappings, and mobilization against the government. Yet, even official governmental and political leaders from the Niger Delta states emphasize that they have been marginalized for years and need affirmative action to redress developmental concerns. The main states involved are Delta, Rivers, Akwa Ibom, and Bayelsa.[31]

According to Kingsley Akeni, "[I]n recent years, the communities in the Niger Delta region practically play host to a multiplicity of armed groups,

---

31. For background, see Olayiwola 'Layi Abegunrin, "The Crisis in the Niger Delta of Nigeria," public workshop on Nigeria, March 22, 2006, United States Institute of Peace, Washington, D.C. Also, "Strategies for Peace in the Niger Delta," Briefing, December 2005, United States Institute of Peace, Washington, D.C. For news accounts, see "How Hostages Were Freed," *Vanguard Newspaper*, March 28, 2006. Also "Blood and Oil," *New York Times*, editorial, April 16, 2006.

cults, confraternities and other social vices creating security concerns. Observers have however maintained that the situation is instigated and exacerbated by the presence of oil and gas activities that encourage the divide-and-rule policy that fuels conflicts in the region. They further emphasize that the emergence of warlords and militias in the area is a by-product of the need to gain local control and obtain the privileges from the oil companies in a particular locale."[32]

A similar perspective is expressed by Franklin Ejoh: "Hostage taking is a grievous and violent action for the expression of some group of people in the Niger Delta as a result of marginalization. . . . This happens when the host communities feel that they are not being recognized [as] the source of wealth to the nation. Neglect by the oil/gas companies and federal government is the major cause. [It is] a situation whereby the host community is being denied social amenities such as good roads, portable pipe-born water, schools, scholarship, employment opportunities, electricity."[33]

A more sinister explanation is found in the enormous wealth being drained off from the oil pipelines through "bunkering." This is a sophisticated operation, since it requires getting the oil offshore and into tankers, which then head to the spot markets of Rotterdam. There are many Nigerian insiders who claim that retired (or even active-duty) military officers are involved in this business, especially officers from the Ijaw-speaking areas. The billions of dollars thus received from illegal bunkering are plowed back into advanced weapons, which abound.

Despite the arrest and projected trials of such MEND leaders as Alhaji Asari Dokubo on grounds of treason for encouraging the breakup of Nigeria and partitioning the Delta as a sovereign state, a political settlement is needed to deal with underlying issues. And despite the frequent claims against Alhaji Dokubo as a front for sinister international Muslim networks, there is no public evidence of Muslim involvement in MEND, which is primarily an Ijaw ethnic organization.

Nigerian military responses to partition movements in the Delta have tended to provoke backlashes and unintended consequences. During the Abacha military regime, the government hung Ken Sara Wiwa and others in November 1995, which led to the hardening of the Ogoni ethnic separatist movement as well as the suspension of Nigeria from the British Commonwealth. Since 1999, when locals attacked Nigerian police or military elements, the reprisals have been heavy handed; in one case, an entire village was wiped out.

---

32. Kingsley Akeni, "Demobilisation and Reintegration of Armed Groups in the Niger Delta," *PeaceWorks News* 6, no. 1, (May 2006) 5.

33. Franklin Ejoh, "Hostage Taking in the Niger Delta," *PeaceWorks News* 6, no. 1 (May 2006).

The need for political leadership from the south-south within a united Nigeria is obvious. The fact that the new vice president, Goodluck Jonathan, is Ijaw and from Bayelsa is seen as a strategic move by the PDP. President Yar'Adua has called for a Marshall-type plan in the Delta to address basic needs. If the federal government were to impose a state of emergency in the Delta as it did in Plateau State in 2004, it would have consequences throughout the country. Imposition of military rule in the areas of turmoil would serve as a symbol of top-down centralization and might lead to another civil war. Such a war in the mangrove swamps of the Delta, particularly with complex ethnolinguistic factors at play, would be a civil and ecological nightmare for Nigeria and for the international community.

Democratic Federalism

The challenge of democratic process building in Nigeria is to move the focus from personalities to institutions at all levels. Any deviation from regional rotation agreements (and the 1999 Nigerian constitution) would probably result in political turmoil. Most important, democratic practice requires respecting constitutional limits on power. In a state driven by oil revenues with a legacy of military rule as in Nigeria, the idea of term limits is crucial to the expectation that power is not absolute. Furthermore, Nigeria is a three-tier federation, with a presumption of decentralized or balanced power. Has a new cohort of leaders emerged from the 2007 elections to deal with the challenges of nation building in Nigeria? How does the presumption of north-south rotation of leadership impact the capacity to deal with political challenges?

At a macro level, many in Nigeria acknowledge that power sharing between the northern (Muslim) and southern parts of the country requires some form of presidential rotation if the country is to stay together. With the transition from military to civilian rule in 1999, northerners were key in voluntarily shifting power to the southwest (and Obasanjo). But there was an understanding—the so-called gentlemen's agreement—that power and the presidency would shift back to the north in the next election.

Yet, in the buildup to the 2007 elections, many voices in the southeast and south-south—apart from the partition voices—were arguing that it was their turn for the presidency. The northern states, which constitute a majority in the country (nineteen out of thirty-six states), insisted that national unity required a northern president in 2007 (and a presumed vice president from the southeast or south-south).

If President Obasanjo had managed a credible political transition in 2007, he would have enhanced the African Statesmen Initiative, an effort launched by former African leaders who met in Bamako, Mali, in summer 2005 to enable African presidents who have lost elections, or respected their term limits, to rise to the status of continental "elders" in promoting democratic pathways. No genuine African statesman, or stateswoman, wants to leave the legacy of a failed state.[34]

If a Vision 2010 scenario were developed for a political pathway toward a more democratic federal system in Nigeria after the 2007 elections, the benchmarks would probably be these: inclusive cabinets form at various levels but without obviating the need for a robust opposition; election tribunals function and are seen as fair and effective; the federal government makes every effort to gain domestic legitimacy, especially in the Delta region; the election reform commission evaluates the lessons to apply them to the next political cycle starting in 2010 in preparation for elections in 2011. Obviously, miscalculations could occur at any point in this cycle. The larger question is whether Nigeria is headed toward a single-party system, with only token opposition elements. If single-party domination prevails, how will the country handle the many challenges outlined in this monograph?

---

34. While Obasanjo has stepped down from the presidency, he is still the all-powerful chairman of the PDP. While he is based at his farm in Otta, Abeokuta (Ogun State), apparently he intends to pursue an advanced degree in Christian theology from a religious institution in Lagos.

5

U.S. Relations with Nigeria

Over the years, there has been extensive interaction between Americans and Nigerians both at the official and nonstate levels. For purposes of this monograph, several categories of relations are relevant: military and security; diplomatic and political; economic, business, and educational; cultural, religious, and nongovernmental.[1]

Military and Security Relations

The United States has two major security concerns in Nigeria, both related to the underlying issue of system stability: turmoil in the oil-producing areas of the Delta and potentially disruptive extremist religious elements in the north.[2] Some of the Delta issues, including U.S. naval power offshore, have been mentioned previously. The issue of extremist religious elements revolves around the so-called Taliban, not only in Nigeria but also elsewhere in Africa.[3] Clearly, al-Qaeda affiliates have been present in East Africa (for example, in Kenya and Tanzania), the Horn of Africa (especially Somalia), North Africa (notably Morocco and Algeria), and some urban areas of South Africa. The question as to whether there are extremist elements in West Africa, which has been relatively immune from radical Islamist factions, has become more prominent.

---

1. For an overview of U.S. relations with Africa, including contemporary Nigeria, see Sulayman S. Nyang, "US-Africa Relations over the Last Century: An African Perspective," *Social Research* 72, no. 4 (winter 2005): 913ff. Nyang notes that after 9/11 Africans had "a sense of shock and sympathy for the families of the victims. But . . . there were tiny pockets of African opinions that gave theological and political interpretations to the events . . . [and] that certain elements in countries such as Nigeria showed some solidarity with Osama bin Laden. This was certainly not the position of President Olusegun Obasanjo and his government. It is clear, however that 9/11 and its aftermath further polarized some of these African societies where the ongoing struggles between the Islamic and Christian fundamentalist cartels received reinforcement from America's war against international terrorism. Because all politics is local, [these] cartels have exploited and will continue to exploit local fears and local interests to create a global sense of solidarity among their African co-religionists and collaborators."
2. On Delta issues, see Paul M. Lubeck, Michael J. Watts, and Ronnie Lipschutz, *Convergent Interests: U.S. Energy Security and the "Securing of Nigerian Democracy,"* International Policy Report (Washington, D.C.: Center for International Policy, February 2007).
3. See Soji Akomolafe, "Nigeria, the United States and the War on Terrorism: The Stakes and the Stance," in *Nigeria in Global Politics*, 225–44; Fola Soremekun, "The 911 Incident and Its Aftermath: Implications for Nigeria-U.S. Relations," in *Nigeria in Global Politics*, 245–64, and Olayiwola Abegunrin, "Nigerian Foreign Policy under the Obasanjo Administration, 1999–2005," in *Nigeria in Global Politics*, 265–76.

Within the West African context, U.S. security officials need to understand the history and cultures of the region so as not to overreact to issues such as the sharia movement or the legitimate debates going on within components of the ummah as Nigerians respond to globalization and modernization. Also, clearly different patterns and legacies prevail in countries as diverse as Senegal and Nigeria.

The June 2005 issue of the *African Terrorism Bulletin*, published by the Institute for Security Studies (ISS), a nonprofit research organization based in South Africa and funded by the Norwegian Agency for Development Co-operation, focuses on western Africa and, in particular, highlights reports from the Belgian-based International Crisis Group (ICG) released in March 2005.[4] The issue analyzes the United States' Pan Sahel Initiative (PSI) and cautions that the presence of U.S. Special Forces in the area may provoke political backlash. It also discusses the U.S. Department of Defense's Trans-Saharan Counterterrorism Initiative (TSCI):

> The US is to launch the Trans Saharan Counterterrorism Ini-tiative (TSCI) in June 2005. The TSCI is built on the experiences of the earlier Pan Sahel Initiative (PSI), which provided training and equipment to light infantry companies in Mali, Mauritania, Chad and Niger. The new initiative will kick off with Exercise Flintlock 2005, in which US special operation forces will train their counterparts in military tactics, which they deem critical in enhancing regional security and stability. The new program has more funding available; it will receive about $100 million a year for five years, and a wider scope, adding Morocco, Alge-ria, Tunisia, Senegal and Nigeria to the original four countries in the PSI. Notable is the inclusion of Nigeria, the continent's big-gest petroleum producer and source of one-fifth of all-American oil imports. A US defense official labeled the new initiative an

---

4. According to the article "Islamic Terrorism in the Sahel: Fact or Fiction," the ICG report "suggests that a heavy-handed US approach to fighting terrorism in the Sahel would risk what it aims to prevent: a rise of Islamist militancy. The report hones in on the countries of the Sahel including Mauritania, Mali, Niger and Chad. These countries are perceived to be vulnerable to terrorist activity. . . . The countries of the Sahel are among the poorest in the world. They face a constant battle against developmental challenges, and Western donors and particularly the US are concerned about issues relating to weak governance, security lax border controls, an abundance of small arms and ammunition and a perceived growth of what is termed as 'Islamic activity.' " In addition, "The report finds that the Sahel deserves greater international attention; but not the sort of attention displayed in the initial US response to the perceived threat of terrorism, the Pan Sahel Initiative (PSI). The initia-tive is described as constituting little more than a hunt for terrorists in the region and a series of programs for training African militaries; while some Sahelian governments have used anti-terrorism measures as a pretext to act against their political opposition. It goes on to disapprove of military aid as the only response to this security threat. . . . It is hoped that the new US program, the Trans-Saharan Counter Terrorism Initiative, will incorpo-rate more than military capacity-building to the underdeveloped nations of the Sahel." See http://www.isa.org.za or terrorism@issct.org.za.

important step in the US "War on Terror," with an emphasis on prevention rather than reaction. Recommendations suggesting a broader development approach towards the Sahel by the International Crisis Group and others seem to have been ignored in the TSCI. However, the US Defense Department has said that other US government agencies would become active players in the program at a later stage.[5]

Clearly, the funding levels and organizational links of the U.S. Department of Defense make the TSCI a major development.[6] The ICG cautions regarding heavy-handed military solutions, however, which will be of concern to both U.S. and Nigerian citizens. Meanwhile, an antiterrorism bill was introduced in the Nigerian National Assembly in August 2005—and later passed—that states "any person who does or threatens to do or does an act preparatory to or in furtherance of an act of terrorism or omits to do anything that is reasonably necessary to prevent an act of terrorism or assists or facilitates the activities of persons engaged in an act of terrorism commits an offence." Violators would face five to thirty-five years imprisonment.[7]

Until recently, the U.S. Senate restricted the links between U.S. and Nigerian military units. In spring 2006 earlier sanctions imposed by a measure introduced by Sen. Russell Feingold (D-WI) were lifted, but those imposed by an earlier bill introduced by Sen. Patrick Leahy (D-VT) and linked to cooperation on the extradition of Charles Taylor to Liberia remained in place and hence limited military-to-military educational programs. With the capture of Charles Taylor on March 29, 2006, in Borno, following his escape from Nigerian-provided guest facilities in Port Harcourt and his subsequent return to Liberia—and later to

---

5. Ibid.
6. It is difficult to calculate the actual amount of U.S. military aid that has been proposed, authorized, or expended for use in counterterrorism in Nigeria or elsewhere. See "$100 Million in Anti-Terror Military Aid Urged," *Washington Post*, April 8, 2006.
7. See "Anti-Terrorism Bill Underway," *ThisDay*, August 31, 2005. Thus, "Nigeria would soon have a bill aimed at combating terrorism and related matters as the Federal Executive Council (FEC) yesterday considered and ratified a draft bill that would soon be passed to law by the National Assembly. . . . It describes the act of terrorism to be 'attacks upon a person's life which may cause death, attacks upon the physical integrity of a person, kidnapping of a person, extensive destruction to a government or public facility, a transport system, an infrastructure facility, including an information system, a fixed platform located on the continental shelf, a public place or private property likely to endanger human life or result in major economic loss.

The minister, while shedding more light on the draft bill, emphasized that 'this is not an imposition by the United States government. The incidences of terrorism recorded all over the world is not in the United States alone. You go to the Middle East, North America, Europe, even in some parts of Africa. Do not forget that even before 9/11, there was the embassy incident in Kenya and another African country. . . . Therefore, it behooves on each of these countries to domesticate the law in their respective countries and then they do this through an appropriate Act of the National Assembly. And on this occasion, the Federal Executive Council considered this draft bill which seeks to prevent, prohibit and combat every conceivable act of terrorism and financing of terrorism in Nigeria,' he said."

The Hague—to face charges of crimes against humanity in Sierra Leone, the Leahy sanctions appear to be in the process of being lifted.[8]

In 2007 the *Economist* reported, "A new American command for Africa, known as AFRICOM, will for the first time co-ordinate all the superpower's various military deployments on the continent under a unified command. This, says General William Ward, one of the men in charge of setting up the new command, is 'a recognition of the increasing and growing importance of Africa'—mainly due to terrorists and oil."[9]

The *Economist* continued, stating that

> American concern about terrorism in Africa is sharpened by a growing need for African oil. Nigeria is the continent's biggest exporter of oil to America. The fact that half of its population of about 140m is Muslim worries American counter-terrorist experts. Nigeria already faces an insurgency—not, so far, connected to Muslim grievances—in its oil-rich Delta region. . . . One genuine threat is posed by a group now calling itself al-Qaeda in the Islamic Maghreb—AQIM in American military shorthand. . . . The Americans worry that AQIM may link up with murkier groups, such as the Black Taliban of northern Nigeria. The group was blamed for an attack in April in the city of Kano. This killed scores of people. But the Black Taliban's guilt has been hard to confirm. . . . In general, West Africa has practiced a tolerant and peaceful Islam. But Muslim fundamentalists under the banner of Salifism are certainly becoming more active in the region. . . . The budget of the Trans-Sahara Counter-Terrorism Partnership for 2007 is about $115m, while non-military assistance increased by about 60% last year as well. Unimaginable in many parts of the world, there is keen competition among African countries to host AFRICOM's new headquarters.[10]

Despite the flurry of activities regarding potential military cooperation, as of 2007 the U.S. role in Nigeria appears to be limited to providing training for

---

8. See "Nigeria to Give up Charles Taylor," *BBC News*, March 25, 2006. Coincidentally, Taylor was captured in Borno just prior to the White House meeting between presidents Bush and Obasanjo. See "A War Criminal Escapes: The Man Who Let Him Go Is Due at the White House This Morning," editorial, *Washington Post*, March 29, 2006.

9. "Africa and the 'War on Terror': Policing the Undergoverned Spaces," *Economist*, June 16, 2007, 55–56.

10. Ibid. For more details, see "Pentagon Hopes to Expand Aid Program: Legislation Would Help Foreign Governments' Military Security Forces," *Washington Post*, May 13, 2007. According to this article, "Legislation sent to Capitol Hill—under the title of Building Global Partnerships Act of 2007—would allow the secretary of defense 'with the concurrence of the secretary of state,' to spend up to $750 million to help foreign governments build up not only their military forces, but also police and other 'security forces' to 'combat terrorism and enhance stability.'" Nigeria is listed as one of the "coalition partners."

peacekeeping purposes. There has been a strong backlash in Nigeria against the idea of a U.S. African command, and efforts have been made to discourage an AFRICOM headquarters in West Africa. Yet, as the United Nations prepares to take a more active role in assisting the African Union in Darfur (Sudan), there may be more training and support activities.[11] The issue of security cooperation in the Gulf of Guinea remains an open question, which requires a range of capacities and skills.[12] As of 2007, Nigeria has not accepted U.S. offers of assistance on coastal security.

The situation in the Niger Delta, adjacent to the Gulf of Guinea, is regarded by the U.S. as an internal Nigerian affair. U.S. ambassador to Nigeria John Campbell, in a news conference with journalists in March 2006, expressed sympathy with the Niger Delta people with regard to development and indicated that once hostages were released, the U.S. would seek an expanded role in helping to further economic gains there. According to Nigeria's *Daily Independent*,

> He expressed the willingness of his government to support any peaceful initiative that would lead to the release of the two U.S. citizens and a Briton that are held hostage by militants and the resolution of the Niger Delta crisis. He disclosed that the U.S. was looking forward to the release of the three hostages, stating that once the hostages were released and there were no further hostage taking, his government would be expanding dialogue with the federal, state and local governments with the goal of giving increased assistance to the area. Said he: "The Niger Delta is dear to us. We are deeply concerned about the situation in the Niger Delta. We have sympathy for the legitimate aspiration of the people. Hostage taking is however not justified; we are committed to accelerating assistance if there are no more hostages and we are supportive of measures to alleviate the suffering of the people."
>
> The ambassador also denied any knowledge of request from Nigerian government for military assistance in tackling the Niger Delta crisis. "America has not received any request from Nigeria for military assistance. The Niger Delta is an internal matter and we expect the Nigerian government to deal with it," he said. [13]

But the lack of security in the Delta region, kidnappings, the loss of production capacity, and the quality of leadership necessary to resolve

---

11. See "Sudan: The UN May Send Troops, Eventually," *Economist*, June 16, 2007, 54. The *Economist* noted, "Finally, after almost a year of negotiations, Sudan's government has agreed to let a 'hybrid' African Union (AU) and UN peacekeeping force be sent to its ruined western region of Darfur."

12. The use of military resources as a default position on such policy matters suggests the old adage, "If you are a hammer, everything looks like a nail."

13. See "We're Watching Nigeria over Third Term—US," *Daily Independent*, March 17, 2006.

these issues all are of vital concern to the United States. According to the *Economist,* the biggest winners of the region are the militants who, claiming to fight for the Delta's poor citizens, conduct kidnappings and create havoc, despite efforts by the president to put forward his own Marshall Plan: "The American Energy Department reckons Nigeria has lost $16 billion in revenue since December 2005. Mr. Yar'Adua says he has a 'Marshall Plan' for the delta up his sleeve and that his new deputy, Goodluck Jonathan, a state governor from there, will play a big part in settling the unrest. But the delta's main militant group has already called Mr. Jonathan a traitor. Last week, attackers blew up part of his country home."[14]

Clearly, there is an overlap of U.S. concerns about energy security in the Gulf of Guinea and the domestic issues of turmoil in the Niger Delta. Given the sensitivities of most Nigerians to the issue of U.S. military involvement in their country, the role of diplomacy becomes paramount. To what extent is the U.S. at full strength in the diplomatic realm?

Diplomatic and Political Relations

With the U.S. preoccupied in Iraq and Afghanistan, and with the global war on terrorism active in other areas, an unfortunate hiatus in high-level diplomatic engagement with Nigeria emerged in 2003–04. U.S. ambassador Howard Jeter had left Nigeria in July 2003. Another career foreign service officer was selected to replace him soon after and confirmed by the U.S. Senate in August, but medical issues subsequently made it impossible for him to take up the post. The process of selection began again. Finally, Ambassador John Campbell, who had previously served in Nigeria under Ambassador Princeton Lyman, was chosen and sworn in on May 18, 2004, arriving in Nigeria on May 20. Both Jeter and Campbell are professional, experienced career foreign service officers (FSOs) and are highly regarded. Yet, this ten-month hiatus, with only a U.S. chargé d'affaires in Abuja, has been symptomatic of low levels of U.S. attention to diplomatic priorities in a country that has been defined as one of the two U.S. anchors in Africa.[15]

This leadership gap has been coupled with the slow move of U.S. embassy facilities from Lagos to Abuja, the earlier closure of the U.S. consulates in Kano and Kaduna, the difficulty of getting young FSOs to volunteer for Nigeria, and the long delays in processing Nigeria visa applications. In addition, while English is the language of the political elite in Nigeria, there has been little incentive or interest in having young FSOs learn Nigerian languages,

---

14. See "Nigeria: New Government, Old Problems," *Economist,* May 26, 2007, 52.
15. Ambassador Campbell completed his tour and left Nigeria in summer of 2007. His confirmed successor, Robin Sanders, arrived in Abuja in late fall, 2007. This again left the U.S. embassy in Abuja with only a chargé d'affaires for several months.

especially Hausa, which is the lingua franca in the north (and throughout much of West Africa).[16]

Under the leadership of Ambassador Campbell, Hausa language training has received more attention at the embassy. And as of 2007, Hausa is being taught at the National Foreign Affairs Training Center in Arlington, Virginia. Also, a 2007 initiative by the United States to support Hausa-speaking schools in the north is a conceptual breakthrough, since Hausa is clearly the language of the people. In addition, Campbell has established U.S. reading rooms in each of the thirty-six states in Nigeria. Staffed by Nigerians, these reading rooms include Internet facilities and may make it easier to expedite links with U.S. educational institutions.

Challenges remain in attracting U.S. staff to Abuja embassy posts, including the tight housing market, water shortages, and ubiquitous electricity failures. This has led the U.S. Department of State to classify Abuja as a "30 percent differential post." Lagos remains at 25 percent. Yet, the difficulties of life in Abuja are less than in most parts of the country, and the real challenge is to get embassy personnel moving around in all thirty-six states of the federation. Otherwise, there is a tacit confirmation of the centralization of activities in the capital city to the possible neglect of long-term needs for a decentralized federalism.

Given these logistical and strategic challenges, the recommendations of the United States Institute of Peace in its special report titled *Political Islam in Sub-Saharan Africa: The Need for a New Research and Diplomatic Agenda* are quite pointed. The report emphasizes the need to better understand political Islam in an African context and to give greater priority to diplomatic activities in Muslim areas of Africa. The report also warns the United States against getting involved in mosque-state (or church-state) relations in African countries.[17]

A key challenge in U.S.-Nigerian relations is to facilitate the visa process so that key political leaders, as well as students and scholars, can interact with their U.S. counterparts. Most U.S. visa processing still occurs in Lagos, which makes it especially difficult for northerners. Security checks require long lead times. In 2007, new regulations required finger printing for all applicants. Even at senior levels a problem remains. Thus, for example, in August 2005, a delegation of Nigerian senators was to have spoken at the Center for Strategic and International Studies in Washington, D.C., but the event had to be postponed because of U.S. visa problems. In addition, courteous treatment of Nigerian visitors (especially those with Muslim names) by Department of

---

16. Even at the state level, Hausa is increasingly used as a "second language" in official business. See "Bauchi Assembly Adopts Hausa as Second Language," *Sunday Independent*, June 22, 2007.

17. See *Political Islam in Sub-Saharan Africa: The Need for a New Research and Diplomatic Agenda*, Special Report 140 (Washington, D.C.: United States Institute of Peace Press, May 2005).

Homeland Security officials once they have entered the United States should be a high priority. The confusion over common Muslim names has led to numerous mix-ups at U.S. domestic airports with Transportation Security Administration personnel, involving, in some cases, senior Nigerian officials. Clearly, policies are only as effective as the people who implement them.

In short, the flow of people and ideas should be encouraged rather than restricted. Interactions between Nigerian Muslims and U.S. citizens is essential to better understanding. Diplomatic and political will must be generated to facilitate this process. Since the U.S. Department of State is responsible for issuing visas, the security procedures need to be streamlined to avoid backlash and resentment.

In addition, the question of religion in U.S.-Nigerian relations should be discussed in a straightforward but nonintrusive manner. Madeleine Albright makes this point in her recent book on religion and world affairs where she discusses many Nigerian issues, such as Christian-Muslim strife, sharia law, and her warm reception by the emir of Kano. She focuses specifically on Kano in its role as part of the indigenous northern Nigerian caliphate.[18]

Finally, the question of U.S. concerns about the political processes in Nigeria needs to be handled in a frank yet diplomatic manner. Central issues in this regard have been the presidential third-term initiative (see chapters 2 and 3), election fraud in 2007 (see chapter 4), and corruption.[19] Regarding the third-term issue, Ambassador Campbell has remarked, "Should Nigeria choose to amend its constitution, we are closely watching how it goes. It should be transparent and according to the rule of law."[20]

Retired U.S. diplomats have been more forthcoming on the third-term issue. According to a 2005 Nigerian news report, "The rumoured third term agenda by President Olusegun Obasanjo took centre stage in public debate in Washington D.C. on Saturday with two former United States ambassadors— Mr. Herman Cohen and Mr. Howard Jeter—warning that the government should not brook the idea. While Cohen, a former US assistant secretary of state, said it would be immoral to amend the 1999 Constitution for Obasanjo to remain in office beyond 2007, Jeter, a former US Ambassador to Nigeria, said any extension plans could undermine the President's stature."[21] Additionally, former ambassador Princeton Lyman coauthored a *Wall Street Journal* editorial

18. *The Mighty and the Almighty: Reflections on America, God, and World Affairs* (New York: HarperCollins, 2006). See pp. 259–64 specifically for her discussion of Kano.

19. Regarding corruption, see Larry Luxner, "Nigerian Envoy Seeks to Repair 'Uneasy Friendship' with U.S." *Washington Diplomat*, August 2006, 15ff. According to Nigerian ambassador Obiozor, "We have seen both the abuse of resources and the positive use of resources. The most important thing is that today, we are wiser in handling such a windfall and using it toward our own development."

20. "We're Watching Nigeria over Third Term—U.S." *Daily Independent*, March 17, 2006.

21. "Third Term Bid's Immoral—ex-US Envoys; Northern Leaders Move against Agenda," *The Punch*, November 21, 2005.

in April 2006 condemning the third-term option.²² Even the G-8 nations were concerned about the potentially negative example of violating the two-term limit in Nigeria.²³

As the Nigerian election season unfolded in 2006–07, U.S. diplomatic and political observers watched carefully for signs of a free and fair process. Flagrant abuses have certainly been chronicled in the international press, through ubiquitous Internet accounts, and in diplomatic interactions between appropriate officials.²⁴ On both sides of the diplomatic street, it is a fact of globalization that the whole world is watching. Generating the good-

---

22. Peter Lewis and Princeton Lyman, "Nigeria on the Edge," *Wall Street Journal*, April 3, 2006. Thus, "The Nigerian government's efforts to restore stability and combat corruption are all placed in jeopardy by the controversy surrounding the president's tenure. Anti-corruption efforts in the Niger Delta are seen locally as part of a political agenda to strengthen the president's camp. In the Muslim-majority northern states, ethnic and religious rivalries have been stoked by concerns over a third presidential term, which would prolong the control of southern politicians...If the People's Democratic Party engineers a heavy-handed attempt to extend Mr. Obasanjo's tenure, or distorts the results of the elections, democracy will certainly be imperiled. Nigeria's fractious public will react angrily to a perception that power is being seized by a strongman president or a single party. Politicians and voters will draw the conclusion that rules are irrelevant, and that politics is merely a brazen grab for power and spoils. Nigeria's contentious ethnic groups, who continue to see some promise in competitive elections and power-sharing, will be polarized by an entrenchment of power.

"Nigeria's fate is of great importance to the U.S. Losing Nigeria's strong voice for democracy and security would reverberate across Africa. If it descends into political turmoil, there are prospects of worsening violence and radicalism throughout the country. This is an important moment for U.S. leaders to champion constitutional rule and orderly democratic succession in Nigeria."

23. See "Obasanjo May Not Attend Next G8 Summit," *Guardian* (Lagos and Abuja), April 30, 2006. Thus, "the current leadership of the G8 is not keen on inviting the President. Sources say the G8 action may be connected to the current political heat being generated in Nigeria over the third term plot; and the likely fallout on the African continent, which bothers many of the developed countries. Since 2002 in Canada, a number of African countries' leaders including Obasanjo had been a regular feature at the G8 summit. It was so at the Evian, France summit of 2003, Sea Island in the United States in 2004 and last year in Gleneagles, United Kingdom. . . . The likelihood of the exclusion of Nigeria's President is being considered in diplomatic circles as both a slap on the country's leadership on the continent, and President Obasanjo himself, considering his towering influence, especially in the last two years as AU chairman. . . . Obasanjo's rating among G8 countries is reportedly dipping due to the likelihood of the extension of his tenure in violation of the two term limit—one of the cardinal principles of a new Africa, which is being sold to the world."

24. See "Nigeria: New Government, Old Problems," *Economist*, May 26, 2007. Thus, "As the gruff, short-tempered and evangelical Mr. Obasanjo leaves office and the mild-mannered, reclusive and devoutly Muslim Mr. Yar'Adua moves in, the big question is how much authority the new man will bring to bear on Africa's most populous nation (of 140m or so), one of the most ungovernable on the planet. The elections that brought Mr. Yar'Adua to office last month were so badly run and marred by such widespread rigging that they lacked even a pretence of democratic plausibility. While opposition groups have filed petitions to annul the results, an outcome unlikely to happen because of Nigeria's tortuously slow legal process, Mr. Yar'Adua may find that the failings of his own party are largely responsible for his doubtful legitimacy. Many Nigerians see Mr. Yar'Adua, who has little experience of the world beyond his northern state of Katsina, as a puppet of Mr. Obasanjo, a tough paternalist and former military ruler who is due to become chairman of the ruling People's Democratic Party (PDP) after the inauguration."

will necessary for such candor is part of the challenge for diplomatic professionals.

Of perhaps even more importance to U.S.-Nigerian political and diplomatic relations is the question of how the United States should try to understand and respond to religious affairs and issues, especially in conflict-prone situations. In July 2007, the Center for Strategic and International Studies published a study, *Mixed Blessings: U.S. Government Engagement with Religion in Conflict-Prone Settings*, with support from the Henry Luce Foundation. Nigeria is a major part of this study. This report tries to get beyond the particulars of religious conflict and suggests a more conceptual framework, including issues of culture. The bottom line is that U.S. diplomats and political analysts need to engage more effectively on these issues rather than just sticking to the diplomatic staples of economics and politics.[25] One step in this direction was the New York symposium titled "Religious Conflict in Nigeria" held by the Council on Foreign Relations (CFR) on May 8, 2007. Issues of Muslim-Christian relations in Nigeria were a central part of these discussions.[26] CFR is undertaking a broader program on issues of religious conflict and U.S. foreign policy.

Economic, Business, and Educational Relations

As mentioned previously, many U.S. businesses have been reluctant to engage in Nigeria because of the high levels of corruption and consequent possible liability under the U.S. Foreign Corrupt Practices Act of 1977. Even some of the large U.S. oil-related corporations, such as Kellogg, Brown and Root (KBR), an engineering and construction company, have been embarrassed by allegations of "facilitation payments," or bribes. (A KBR corporate counsel was quoted in the Nigeria media as saying, "Everyone does it!")

Nigerian regulatory requirements may also be an impediment, given the long delays for approvals. On the other hand, many international companies take advantage of the ambiguities of the Nigerian situation to ignore

---

25. The project codirectors are Rick Barton and Karin von Hippel; the lead author was Liora Danan and the contributing author was Alice Hunt. Chapter 4 deals with a Nigerian case study and focuses on diplomacy, humanitarian/development, and security. Chapter 6 deals with recommendations, including issues of culture, conceptualization, and capacity.

26. The CFR symposium was organized and chaired by Walter Russell Mead and Tim Shah. The author participated on the Muslim-Christian dialogue panel along with Father Matthew Kukah. In November 2007, CFR sponsored the visit of the Sultan of Sokoto and his entourage to New York and Washington, D.C. The sultan addressed the council on "Islam and Democracy in Nigeria." Throughout his trip, he made the point that Islam and democracy are compatible. The sultan also made the point that there are no extremists in Islam, that is, if people are extremists, they are not true Muslims.

or avoid compliance, even when such compliance is warranted.[27] The case of Pfizer drug testing in Kano in 1996, allegedly without authorization, had subsequent implications because many Kano parents resisted having their children inoculated against polio during the Fourth Republic period. In 2007 the state government of Kano lodged a lawsuit against Pfizer for several billion U.S. dollars on behalf of Kano parents who had lost their children in the drug tests.[28]

The Corporate Council on Africa (CCA), based in Washington, D.C., works with counterpart groups in Nigeria—for example, the Manufacturers Association of Nigeria (MAN) and the Nigerian Association of Chambers of Commerce, Industry, Mines and Agriculture (NACCIMA). CCA also works with U.S. companies engaged (or considering engagement) in Nigeria and encourages exchange delegations of business and political leaders.

Those U.S. companies that are well established in Nigeria tend to remain, while new arrivals tend to be scarce. At the same time, the global economy and, in particular, China's accession to the World Trade Organization (WTO) in December 2001 have created new forms of competition both for U.S. and Nigerian firms. For example, the textile industry in Kaduna, which has supplied much of West Africa with low-cost fabrics, has found it hard to keep up with the Chinese alternatives, either legal or smuggled. (In fall 2007, the major textile factory in Kaduna closed, laying off four thousand workers.) Kano's dominance in light industry is also being challenged by cheap Chinese goods.[29]

---

27. See, for example, "Halliburton Operates without License—NNRA," *Daily Independent*, November 8, 2005.

28. See "Panel Faults Pfizer in '96 Clinical Trial in Nigeria: Unapproved Drug Tested on Children," *Washington Post*, May 7, 2006, which reported, "A panel of Nigerian medical experts has concluded that Pfizer Inc. violated international law during a 1996 epidemic by testing an unapproved drug on children with brain infections. That finding is detailed in a lengthy Nigerian government report that has remained unreleased for five years, despite inquiries from the children's attorneys and from the media."

29. See "Obasanjo, Chinese Leader Begin Talks in Abuja Today," *Guardian* (Lagos and Abuja), April 26, 2006. Thus, "Sino-Nigerian relations will receive a boost today as President Olusegun Obasanjo and his Chinese counterpart, President Hu Jintao, brainstorm on social and economic relations between the two nations in Abuja. . . . During the two-day state visit, Hu will address a joint session of the National Assembly as well as the China-Nigeria Business Forum. He will be hosted later to a state banquet by the President. . . . Hu's visit is aimed at consolidating the growing bilateral economic relations with Nigeria. His coming is also to reciprocate Obasanjo's trip to Beijing last year and to equally review the implementation of the agreements reached by them. The two leaders are also expected to sign new economic co-operation agreements in infrastructural development. Hu may use the visit to speak of China's in-road into the Nigerian economy, which reached a climax in last January's acquisition of $2.3 billion majority stake in plum oil fields by the Asian giant's national offshore oil company."

Also see "Nigeria to Establish Air Link with Argentina, China," *ThisDay*, April 28, 2006. Thus, the Aviation Minister "met with the Deputy governor of Chinese Province of Henan who solicited for air links between Nigeria and the Province. . . . He also disclosed that President Obasanjo has granted use of Lagos International Trade Fair to the Henan Province to develop into a special Trade Free Zone."

In new fields, such as satellite technology, Nigeria is working with the Chinese rather than with the Americans.[30]

African agriculture was intended to be helped by the U.S. African Growth and Opportunity Act, but Nigeria in the post–oil boom era has frequently let agricultural cash crops languish. The Nigerian domestic market came to rely increasingly on imports. Yet, even China enters the picture on potential agriculture developments, that is, if Nigeria can organize its export opportunities. According to Vice President Atiku Abubakar, the Chinese have indicated they would buy all the cassava Nigeria can produce in the future![31]

Clearly, the oil industry is the mainstay of Nigerian-U.S. economic relations and will increase in importance as liquefied natural gas comes on stream. President Obasanjo served as his own petroleum minister. Others with a deep knowledge of the oil industry, such as Rilwan Lukman of Kaduna State, have been frustrated by the politics in Nigeria. The highly centralized nature of the oil industry, and its capital intensive rather than labor intensive nature, means that U.S. oil companies tend to work with those at the highest levels of government in Nigeria. The key to oil production is stability, which tends to pull the companies into security-related matters where they are often very uncomfortable. Muhammadu Buhari, currently leader of the opposition in Nigeria, served as petroleum minister in previous administrations and obviously is active in trying to change Nigerian politics.

The key to U.S.-Nigerian business relations is to take advantage of the large number of Nigerians who came to the United States in the 1990s and now have U.S. citizenship. While Nigeria allows dual citizenship, the United States does not. In practice this does not seem to be a deterrent to Nigerian Americans doing business in Nigeria. The most important aspect of this Nigerian-American economic engagement in Nigeria is the regional profile of those involved. During the Abacha regime (1993–98), it was mainly southern Nigerians who came to the United States, often those from the

---

30. See "China Builds and Launches a Satellite for Nigeria," *Washington Post*, May 14, 2007. Thus, "China announced Monday that it had launched a Chinese-manufactured satellite into orbit on behalf of Nigeria, marking the first time China has built a commercial satellite and put it into orbit on contract for another country. . . . Monday's launch of the NIGCOMSAT-1, aboard a Long March 3B rocket, represented more of a commercial challenge, Chinese officials said. The official New China News Agency said China secured the $311 million contract in 2004 in a bidding process in which 21 other companies took part . . . . the new launch was seen as a symbol of China's broad network of economic relations with Africa. . . . China has been particularly eager to establish commercial relations with oil-producing nations such as Nigeria. . . . The launch was hailed by Nigerian officials, however, as a breakthrough in getting away from exclusive reliance on oil. Hammed Rufai, Nigeria's managing director of the NIGCOMSAT-1 project, told the news agency that the satellite will help Nigeria move toward knowledge-based industries. Other officials said Nigeria hopes to sell communications bands to neighboring African countries. . . . The satellite will be managed from a control station in Abuja, the Nigerian capital." Also see "Snubbed by U.S., China Finds Its Own Space Partners," *New York Times*, May 24, 2007.

31. Atiku Abubakar, public lecture at the Woodrow Wilson Center, Washington, D.C., May 2005.

Yoruba-speaking southwest. They tended to be educated professionals who accumulated capital that could be a source for investment in Nigeria. Such diaspora groups follow political as well as economic developments in Nigeria with keen interest.[32]

With the privatization initiatives of President Obasanjo, many of the large Nigerian parastatals (including some aspects of the government-owned oil industry) have been privatized. This has created the impression in northern Nigeria that the United States (including Nigerian Americans) and the Nigerian government favored those from the southwest zone.

At the same time, many northern Nigerians living and working in the United States are in a position to interact economically with Nigeria. Founded in 1991, the Zumunta Association USA "is a progressive non-profit organization of Northern Nigerians based in the United States of America. . . . The organization's objectives include helping develop Northern Nigerian states technologically, socially and economically; catering for its members welfare; preserving Nigeria's rich cultural heritage; and improving Nigeria's image globally."[33]

On July 30, 2005, the Zumunta Association held its twelfth annual national convention in Windsor, Connecticut. The scheduled keynote speaker, Muhammadu Buhari, had to cancel at the last minute and was replaced by Mohammed B. Marwa, a businessman and former governor of Lagos and Borno states. Marwa spoke on the topic of technology and development and the role of the Nigerian diaspora. Special guests included numerous high-level Nigerian politicians and business types, both living in Nigeria and abroad. Clearly, the northern Nigerian presence in the United States has attracted significant attention in various Nigerian realms. The extraordinary use of cell phones by northern Nigerians means that there is constant contact between such users in the United States and Nigeria.

An example of the educational link with the United States and northern Nigerians was the efforts of former vice president Atiku Abubakar, who has worked with American University in Washington, D.C., to establish the Abti University in Yola, commonly known as American University, Yola. Students entered in fall term 2005. The focus is on technology and business entrepreneurship and constitutes the first private, American-style university in northern Nigeria. The international recruitment of faculty is being handled by American University.

Other northern Nigerian universities, such as Bayero University in Kano (BUK), Usman Dan Fodio University (UDF) in Sokoto, and Ahmadu Bello University (ABU) in Zaria have extensive U.S. contacts. Significantly,

---

32. See, for example, "Diaspora Nigeria Citizens (DNC) in Africa, Asia-Pacific, Europe and the Americas," c/o NDM, P. O. Box 747, Beltsville, Maryland, 20704-0747, USA, May 24, 2006 letter to various Nigerian leaders, Mobolaji E. Aluko, president of the Nigeria Democratic Movement NDM (USA), ndmmovement@gamji.com.

33. See www.zumunta.org. Note: *zumunta* is the Hausa word for "mutual support."

when the assessment of Nigerian universities was done by the Abuja-based National Universities Commission (NUC) in 2005–06, the two universities in Nigeria tied for first place in the rankings were BUK and UDF. Clearly, northern universities have come of age in all fields of endeavor.

Higher education is a critical component of economic development, and the United States has major comparative advantages in this domain. Many U.S. universities have direct bilateral links with Nigerian universities and have developed long-term forms of trust and cooperation at the human-relations level.[34] Again, visa issues may remain a problem, except at the senior or official levels.

Cultural, Religious, and Nongovernmental Organization Relations

There are an estimated six to seven and a half million American Muslims, about 2 percent of the total U.S. population. According to a 2007 Pew report titled *Muslim Americans: Middle Class and Mostly Mainstream,*

> Unlike Muslim minorities in many European countries, U.S. Muslims are highly assimilated, close to parity with other Americans in income and overwhelmingly opposed to Islamic extremism, according to the first major, nationwide random survey of Muslims. . . . On balance, they believe that Muslims coming to the United States should adopt American customs, rather than trying to remain distinct. And they are even more inclined than other Americans to say that people who want to get ahead can make it if they work hard; 71 percent of U.S. Muslims agreed with that statement, compared with 64 percent of the general public. "What emerges is the great success of the Muslim American population in its socioeconomic assimilation," said Amaney Jamal, an assistant professor of politics at Princeton University who was a senior adviser on the poll. "Given that for the past few years they've been dealing with the backlash from 9/11, these numbers are extremely impressive."[35]

Many observers see these patterns as quite distinct from European experiences.[36]

---

34. See "NUC Sends 10 VCs to Harvard, MIT for Training," www.gamji.com, placed on line by Juliana Taiwo in Abuja, April 19, 2006.

35. See "Survey: U.S. Muslims Assimilated, Opposed to Extremism," *Washington Post*, May 23, 2007.

36. See "Special Report, Islam, America and Europe: Look Out, Europe, They Say. Why So Many Muslims Find It Easier to Be American than to Feel European," *Economist*, June 24, 2006, 29. Yet, also see "Tales from Eurabia: Contrary to Fears on Both Sides of the Atlantic, Integrating Europe's Muslims Can Be Done," *Economist*, June 24, 2006, 11.

More specifically, cultural relations between Nigerians and African-American communities have been deep and extensive. Much of this has involved relations with coastal Nigerians rather than the interior Muslim communities. Yet, the fact that Yoruba communities in the southwest zone are about 50 percent Muslim and 50 percent Christian mixed with traditional believers has blunted some of the religious identity component of this relationship. There is an especially keen interest in American universities and local communities in the Yoruba connection, in part because of the world-class literature coming from that area. In addition, the Yoruba language is still spoken in some of the Gullah islands off Georgia.

At the same time, many from the African-American communities in every major U.S. city have a legacy of West African Muslim roots.[37] The connection with West Africa is profound. Research has shown that some of the early leaders in the Nation of Islam movement in the United States are likely to have had Fulani roots from West Africa. Subsequently, when the Nation of Islam movement split into its core group, plus its more orthodox Sunni incarnation, the latter's ties to Sunni communities in West Africa increased. For example, the pilgrimage to Mecca experience of Malcolm X in 1964 (after which he changed his name to Malik al-Shabazz) was profound.[38]

The links between Nigerian Christians and U.S. counterpart communities have had even greater impact than the U.S.-Muslim connections. This is true not only with the African churches in the United States—such as the increasingly active Yoruba-based Aladura churches—but also with mainstream, evangelical and Pentecostal churches. Visiting American evangelicals, such as Richard Roberts of Oral Roberts University, preach to huge congregations in places such as Ibadan. The historic link between North American evangelicals in the Middle Belt of Nigeria has been mentioned previously. At present, many Nigerian church leaders are trained in the United States and funds from U.S. church groups are often focused on counterparts in Nigeria.

Among the mainstream Nigerian protestant and Catholic churches, there is increasing evidence of interaction with their North American counterparts. In spring 2007 the visits of the head of the Anglican Church in Nigeria, Most Reverend Peter Akinola, who was also serving as head of the Christian Association in Nigeria (CAN), caused considerable controversy. The split in the U.S. Episcopalian community over homosexuality resulted

---

37. See Qamar-ul Huda, *The Diversity of Muslims in the United States: Views as Americans*, Special Report 159 (Washington, D.C.: United States Institute of Peace Press, February 2006). The report focuses on an overview of American Muslim NGOs, the Pew research study on Islamic extremism, the national fatwa condemning terrorism, religious and interfaith organizations, civic and political organizations, legal organizations, the views of American Muslim scholars, and multipronged conflict prevention.

38. As a student, the author was privileged to meet Malcolm X in Ibadan, Nigeria, on his return from Mecca and to hear firsthand the account of his personal transformation after praying next to European Muslims with blue eyes and blond hair.

in a number of U.S. churches placing themselves under the authority of the Nigerian prelate.[39]

After Akinola stepped down as head of the CAN, a new head was selected, the Catholic Archbishop of Abuja, John Onaiyekan. Archbishop Onaiyekan is well known as one of the peacemakers in interfaith dialogue in Nigeria and is highly regarded by Muslim dignitaries.[40] (As noted earlier, he is cochair of NIREC.) He has also served as a liaison with many in the international community.

Significantly, as of June 2007, the two major religious leaders in Nigeria—the president of CAN (John Onaiyekan) and the president of the NSCIA (Sa'ad Abubakar)—both have extensive international experience and are widely recognized as interfaith peacemakers in Nigeria. Yet, as tensions increase between Muslims and Christians in Nigeria, the issue of U.S.-Nigerian relations is not far from the surface. U.S. church groups are especially concerned about some of the sharia laws that have been set up since 2000 in the far northern states of Nigeria. Northern Nigerians are concerned that U.S. political and financial pressures are being stacked against them. With the power shift to the north in 2007, whether these concerns continue may well impact U.S.-Nigerian relations.

Apart from the religious connections between the United States and Nigeria, a wide range of several hundred U.S.-based NGOs is engaged in activities in Nigeria. The types of organizations include those with concerns for women's issues and human rights to groups devoted to health and education issues. Some NGOs are incorporated in Nigeria but have U.S. and international links, including in the area of conflict resolution. One example of an issue on

39. See "Blunt Bishop: How Peter Akinola's Rejection of Liberal 'Sins' Could Push the Anglican Church to Split," *Time*, February 19, 2007, 52. Thus, "The Most Rev. Peter Akinola of Nigeria was in New York City late in January making one of his increasingly frequent forays into what he once would have considered enemy territory. . . . The image could be described as unintentionally double-edged. To a significant number of critics, far from bridging a gap, Akinola, 63, is actively involved in widening one. As primate to 17 million Nigerian Anglicans and head of an African bishop's group with total flock of 44 million, he is one of the most influential leaders in the Anglican Communion, the global 78 million-member confederation that includes the 2.2 million congregants in the Episcopal Church (U.S.A.). Indeed, he is the highest-profile figure in the southward shift of Christianity as a whole. Yet he may exercise that influence by helping pull his communion apart, largely over the issue of the church's stand on homosexuality." Note: His return trip to the United States in April 2007 helped consolidate the split within the U.S. church and aligned those against homosexuality with the Nigerian church.

40. See "Buhari Congratulates New CAN President," *Daily Trust*, June 22, 2007. Thus, All Nigeria Peoples Party presidential candidate, General Muhammadu Buhari has congratulated Dr. John Onaiyekan on his election as the new CAN President. In a letter dated June 20, General Buhari said, "I received with joy and gratitude to Almighty God your election as the National President of the Christian Association of Nigeria (CAN). This victory is indeed well deserved. I have over the years, closely observed your activities as a clergyman and your patriotic state on the socio-political events of our country. Your ability to combine your preaching and practical action with your humility has earned my respect for you. . . . I believe those of us in the political scene will continue to benefit from your wisdom. May God guide you in the service of our fatherland."

the medical front, which has involved NGOs at all levels, has been the issue of vaccinations in the northern Nigerian states. As noted previously, there was an initial reluctance of some northern Nigerian states to cooperate with the international polio vaccine campaign. The resistance to the vaccinations in Kano after 1999 was in part a public reaction to the experience of Pfizer clinical trials in Kano in the mid-1990s, which allegedly were undertaken without the full range of human subject review protections. Kano State sued Pfizer over this issue in 2007. In response, Pfizer claims they had appropriate permissions. Some Kano religious and political leaders felt that the polio vaccines were a way for the West to sterilize their daughters as part of a larger anti-Muslim conspiracy! Subsequently, with the encouragement of Governor Shekarau and the emir of Kano, oral polio vaccines have been administered to the children of Kano. More recently, the new sultan of Sokoto, Sa'ad Abubakar, has also agreed to serve as the national chairman of the polio campaign. But suspicions continue in the north that even basic health precautions may have a "clash of civilizations" dimension.

Clearly, there is a need for broader engagement with the Muslim north to provide the context of trust within which more specific NGO and international governmental organizations (IGOs) can function. Most NGOs are functionally specific but require cooperation at all levels in Nigeria to achieve access and fulfill their missions.

The Future of U.S. Relations with Nigeria

The complexity of U.S.-Nigerian relations is as obvious as is its critical importance. There is the challenge of working at federal, state, and local levels. There is the challenge of building trust as a precondition for other types of specific engagement. There is the challenge of not allowing diaspora factors to unduly influence U.S. policy while encouraging the human links as bridges of understanding.

Since September 11, 2001, military and security forms of engagement have become increasingly important, but they should not take priority over diplomatic and political ties. (Obviously, these dimensions are highly interdependent.) Economic and business ties tend to revolve around the oil industry, and this dimension will increase in significance. The Nigerian diaspora is an increasingly salient factor in building constructive international interactions, but it should not be encouraged to skew relations with the less-well-represented regions in Nigeria. Educational links were dormant during the Abacha era, but they have gained strength since 1999 and represent a major investment in the future. (The need to improve the visa system is critical to this endeavor.) A wealth of cultural, religious, and NGO ties creates the rich texture of linkages that may be productive but may also work at cross-purposes.

From a U.S. policy perspective it is important to set priorities and to see the relationship as a whole and not just as the sum of its very diverse parts. The USAID approach tries to be strategic—within the context of its State Department parent organization—but often is bureaucratic in its functional and project-oriented predispositions. Thus, it may address conflict mitigation as a project, the reduction of HIV/AIDS as a project, democratic governance as a project, the improvement of livelihoods as a project, the increased use of social-sector services as a project, etc,[41] but some of these projects may work at cross-purposes and leave critical gaps in the larger context.

A key to a better understanding of Nigeria from a U.S. perspective is how to get a better grasp of Nigeria's long legacy of connections with the Muslim world. It is this challenge that will enable U.S. policymakers to view Nigeria in its global pivotal role, that is, as a workable bridge between Muslim and Christian communities worldwide and as a link between Western and non-Western cultural zones. The diversity of the United States and the diversity of Nigeria make for a parallel set of underlying challenges in creating unity from diversity, and achieving what both countries seek: from many . . . one.

---

41. See *USAID/Nigeria Country Strategic Plan, 2004–2009* (unrestricted version), 93 pages. For a more recent USAID report, see *Democracy and Governance Assessment of Nigeria* (December 2006), 45 pages. This contracted report deals with democracy and governance problems and prospects, key political actors and their interests, institutional arenas, and strategic and programmatic recommendations. Under key actors, there is a section on "religious groups" (24). Thus, "Religious institutions constitute the widest and deepest expressions of popular participation in Nigeria. Besides Islam and Christianity, syncretism among local and world religions is common. Secret religious cults remain significant forms of organization in the South-South zone, and, in general, because many Nigerians are pragmatic, they take a 'diversified portfolio' approach to selecting religious rituals to solve their needs."

6

Conclusions

Nigeria is one of the most complex countries in the world in terms of its ethnic and religious diversity and its wide range of oil-driven, socioeconomic disparities. The approximate parity in religious identity demographics makes the country a pivotal state within the global context, especially given its large and growing population. The oil boom since the 1970s has allowed for extremes of wealth and has also created opportunities for nation building and interfaith cooperation, often not possible in a non-energy-producing country. For instance, the fast-track relocation of the capital from Lagos to Abuja during the 1980s and 1990s to accommodate a north-south balance of power would not have been possible in most developing countries, although it has been tried with mixed success in Brazil (Brazilia), Tanzania (Dodoma), and Pakistan (Islamabad).

The underlying African context also has historical and cultural realities that are quite distinctive in terms of transnational Muslim linkages. Since the eleventh century, the state of Borno has been oriented to its Chadian and Sudanic east. Since the fifteenth century, Hausa communities in the north have maintained ties with North Africa. Yet, most Nigerian Muslim ties are with West Africa, especially in the Sahelian zone. In recent times, the links with Saudi Arabia have increased considerably, especially through the pilgrimage process but also as a general alliance in stabilizing the international community system. For historical reasons, Nigeria has had less contact with other pivotal states in the Muslim world, such as Egypt, Iran, Pakistan, Turkey, and Indonesia. Obviously, Nigeria shares some commonalities with Egypt and Pakistan through their English-language legacy. London continues to serve as a nexus among all English-speaking pivotal states. Contemporary Muslim identities and organizations in Nigeria range from the grassroots-level Sufi brotherhoods and their more recent challengers (the anti-innovation legalists, such as the Izala) to the more recent student, youth, and women's organizations. National umbrella organizations, often designed on federalist principles to accommodate regional and subnational realities, have tried to create a sense of unity within the ummah across very disparate groups. As such, they tend to be part of the establishment, including traditional rulers and modern-sector professional groups.

Occasionally, there has been a backlash within the Nigerian ummah to the rapid socioeconomic changes. The most violent conflict was in December 1980 and thereafter, between Maitatsine followers based in Kano who drew on pre-Islamic cult practices and Muslim authorities. Maitatsine objected to anything modern or Western during the height of the oil-boom period, including bicycles and wristwatches!

Subsequently, the so-called Shiites (or Ikhwan) have challenged both traditional and secular Muslim authorities, taking their inspiration from the Iranian revolution. The Ikhwan have been a small minority in places like Zaria, Kano, and Sokoto. Yet, they have obvious appeal to a younger generation of semieducated northerners disillusioned with the Muslim establishment and its Sunni legacy. They serve as an international role model with an anti-Western slant and large financial resources. To reach these youths and others, Iran broadcasts an active radio program in Hausa aimed at West Africa, and Ikhwan adherents disseminate English publications in Nigeria. In addition, these youths are attracted to certain aspects of Shia ritual and practice, such as the Ashura festival. And there are the obvious disjunctions created between an Islamic ideal and the rapid changes of the oil-driven economy

More recently, the so-called Taliban network, taking their inspiration from the former Afghan regime, has challenged local- and state-level authorities in the far north, especially in Yobe, Borno, and, more recently, Kano State. The network may be small, but it has shown it can confront the police with armed violence. The Nigerian Taliban has emphasized to local populations that it is not against civilians but only agents of the state. While there is no evidence at this time of an al-Qaeda connection, the vision of setting up a pure Islamic state, as a corrective to the injustices of this world, is an ongoing challenge. This is primarily a "hearts and minds" issue for Nigerians—rather than a military issue—related to the nation-building challenges mentioned throughout this study. Clearly, local governments (and traditional leaders) need to be engaged and develop appropriate responses in order to forestall wider violence. The Nigerian police may fly planes over Kano to try to find the Taliban, but it is hard to imagine that local governments could not have been more actively engaged in the process.

The underlying reality of nation building in West Africa is that national boundaries are porous and historically arbitrary. Nigeria's domestic and transnational domains clearly overlap. Nigeria's capacity for leadership in West Africa and in the larger African context depends not only on official governmental actions but also on the web of nonstate links that characterize the region. Some of these are ethnic, but many are transethnic, especially in the Muslim areas. The legacy of transnational, long-distance trade in places such as Kano may turn out to be a valuable asset as larger economic and political unions are envisioned. Also, the increased links with Mecca and Medina are a natural consequence of centuries of Islamic heritage and the opportunities provided by oil revenues.

Yet, transnational networks within Africa, the Muslim world, and/or within the global economy also raise concerns at all levels in terms of possible extralegal abuses, whether drug trafficking, human trafficking, smuggling, or the potential flow of persons with terrorist intentions. The need for a global vision should be part of public-education endeavors and wise and balanced political leadership, with one foot in the historical cultures of Nigeria and one foot in the twenty-first-century global environment—a new form of Vision 2010.[1]

The Muslim community in Nigeria has historically been committed to the unity of Nigeria since independence in 1960 and to cooperation with non-Muslim compatriots. Despite the sectarian tensions that sometimes emerge, especially in northern Nigeria, the commitment to "keeping Nigeria one" has always prevailed.[2] The central tendency in national politics has been a form of progressive-conservatism, which has been built on the need for cross-regional tolerance and coalitions. The Muslim community in Nigeria is also committed to forms of federalism, ranging from the early regionalism of the First Republic to the thirty-six-state federalism of the Fourth Republic.

This monograph has argued that the five challenges of nation building in Nigeria must be addressed in order to avoid some of the system breakdowns of the past. The top priority is establishing a workable political system. This is not just a matter of formal models, whether borrowed or home grown. It is the challenge of moving toward a system of democratic federalism that is organic to the needs of Nigerians. Whether federal character provisions, or budget allocation formulae, or leadership rotation principles, or other forms of power sharing will be sufficient to ensure an inclusive level playing field remains to be seen. Most important is the sense of fair play, equity, and participation in the national endeavor, including on the religious dimension. This requires leadership. The presidential election of 2007 may have fulfilled the goal of equity between north and south representatives, but it hardly met the goal of fair play.

Rule of law issues are complex in Nigeria. Constitutions in some predominantly Muslim countries often have a boilerplate provision indicating that no law shall contravene sharia. While this formality is not likely in Nigeria, it is also not possible to ignore the sharia legacy in Nigeria. The rule of law, in essence, is one of equality before the law. Political sharia, which is used to target the poor, or women, or the opposition party, is not sharia, which is a way of life, in which the individual and society as a whole are responsible for encouraging justice and fair play. Nigerians will have to debate and craft

---

1. See Mahmud Tukur, *Leadership and Governance in Nigeria: The Relevance of Values* (London: Hodder and Stoughton, 1999). Also, the chapter by Tukur on leadership in Robert I. Rotberg, ed., *Crafting the New Nigeria: Confronting the Challenges* (Boulder, Colo.: Lynne Rienner, 2004).

2. See Matthew Hassan Kukah, *Religion, Politics and Power in Northern Nigeria* (Ibadan: Spectrum Books, 1993). Kukah is a Roman Catholic priest and an active liaison between ethnoreligious communities in Nigeria.

the way in which sharia fits into the larger framework of constitutional law. Meanwhile, the experimentation with multiple jurisprudential systems at the state level is a positive development, assuming that appeals processes are in place to allow redress of grievances and penalty options do not violate international norms, including those within the OIC.

More broadly, rule of law must be seen to apply to the business world and to the electoral process. Since 2004 Nigeria has moved toward a domestic corrupt-practices set of laws that are well intentioned but remain to be tested in the legal system. In terms of electoral law, the election of 2003 was contested in the courts for more than two years before a final verdict was rendered. (The old phrase, "justice delayed is justice denied," comes to mind. The incumbency advantage of delay is obvious.) Yet the acceptance of the Supreme Court decision in July 2005 by the opposition parties speaks well for the emergence of a sense of rule of law. The postelection period after May 29, 2007, takes on special importance in terms of whether legal or extralegal means of redress will be employed. The decision of the Supreme Court in June 2007 to reinstate the former governor of Anambra State—who was only instated by the courts one year before the 2007 election—was widely hailed as a positive assertion of the role of an independent judiciary.[3]

A capacity for conflict mitigation, management, and resolution is crucial. Often this is done through political means and hence the maturity of the political actors is determinative. But the capacity for civil society to enhance mechanisms for conflict mediation also needs to be addressed. These capacities may reside in local NGOs, in educational peace committees, or in the long-term commitment of traditional emirs and chiefs. Obviously, a vibrant sense of rule of law is part of conflict-resolution capacities. But law is only one part. The alternative dispute-resolution mechanisms of mediation and arbitration are perhaps even more salient in the Nigerian context.

The full range of challenges of economic development is beyond the scope of this monograph. Yet in an oil-rich country, the balance between public and private endeavors and the issue of "even" development are central. While some countries—such as China in the 1990s—have allowed coastal areas to develop first, the complex demographics of Nigeria, coupled with the legacy of democratic federalism, have required that interior areas be given equal access to resources and investment. The further challenges of facilitating economic and educational opportunities for the poor and of encouraging the growth of a middle class remain. Clearly, a middle class, however defined, is a necessary component in the other challenges, such as democratic federalism, rule of law, and conflict resolution. If middle-class professionals tend to

---

3. The court reinstated the All Progressive Grand Alliance (APGA) governor rather than the presumed winner of the 2007 election from the PDP.

vote with their feet and move abroad, the economic and political capacities of Nigeria are diminished. How the large Nigerian diaspora will contribute to the economic development of Nigeria remains to be seen.

Part of the hesitation of the diaspora and part of the frustration within lower socioeconomic groups in Nigeria is the sense that corruption is endemic. This is the fifth challenge in nation building and is an especially salient one in an oil economy. The emergence of a super-rich class, with questionable access to government resources, is hardly a portent of social stability. Clearly, political leadership, rule-of-law principles, transparency, and accountability are crucial. The accountability factor is enhanced by a vibrant opposition party and by a free press that can hold governmental feet to the fire and facilitate public scrutiny. The engagement of civil society is the ultimate corrective on abuse of powers, including economic power.

The rapid pace of change in Nigeria makes it hard to project alternative futures. Yet the usual range of scenarios—the good, the bad, and the ugly—should be obvious to governments, corporations, and political leaders. The central question in Nigeria has always been, can (or should) the country stay together?

This monograph has argued that this central question, and the ways Nigerians have answered it, defines Nigeria as a pivotal state. The broader implications of dealing with ethnic and religious diversity are obvious in an African and global context. So far, it seems Nigerians have learned when to pull back from the abyss of civil war, based on their experience in 1967–70. However, the younger generation has no real sense of the horror of that war. Hence, there is a need for elder statesmen to remind and nurture the next generation on the consequences of miscalculation. Clearly, almost all of the older generation of military leaders, including those on the former Biafran separatist side, are committed to Nigerian national unity. Whether they will permit civilian politicians to "make mistakes" affecting national unity remains to be seen. Yet, the willingness of retired military officers to participate in the rough and tumble of civilian politics is a positive sign.

How does this complexity affect U.S.-Nigerian relations? The most obvious advice to the U.S. government would be "do no harm." If Nigeria is pivotal in terms of Muslim-Christian relations, the need to be evenhanded by the U.S. government is obvious. This is complicated by the cross-currents of nongovernmental pressures in the social and political domains on all sides. It is also complicated by the pressures to be proactive on issues of potential terrorism. Since September 11, 2001 (New York and northern Virginia), March 11, 2004 (Madrid), and July 7, 2005 (London), no government will sit back and let terrorists strike and then consider reactive measures. The delicate balance of approaches, ranging from military and police to public education, Track II diplomacy, and nongovernmental mediation, requires far more sensitivity to local realities than is currently evident.

In the long run, local communities in Nigeria will have to take responsibility for their own security issues—hence, the need for the decentralization of police responsibilities in the "serve-and-protect" tradition. This is related to the corruption issue as well. If federal police can be bribed—or if the Nigerian inspector general of police can embezzle large amounts—then local militias or vigilantes will fill the gap and public disillusionment will set in.

The United States needs to engage and normalize its relations with Nigeria at all levels. It must not be pulled into the trap of relying on political actors in Abuja (or in the diaspora) to target those who may turn out to be opposition leaders. The basic requirements for engagement are clear. It should encourage the professional language capabilities of those in the foreign service, especially Hausa, which is the lingua franca in the north; create opportunities for interaction of Americans and Nigerians (including Muslims) through improvements in the visa process; keep the needs of the oil industry in perspective with regard to overall relations; come to grips with the need for deeper understanding of Islam in West Africa, and especially in Nigeria; and set an example of tolerance between people of the book—at home and abroad.

Index

Note on Arabic names: The prefix 'al-' has been retained but ignored when the entry is alphabetized, so that al-Qaeda is listed under Q. 'Bin' is treated as a primary element and appears under B.

About the Author

John N. Paden is Clarence Robinson Professor of International Studies, and professor of Public and International Affairs at George Mason University. He received his B.A. in philosophy from Occidental College, his B.A./M.A. in philosophy, politics, and economics from Oxford University (as a Rhodes Scholar), and his Ph.D. in politics from Harvard University. He has served as Norman Dwight Harris Professor of International Studies and Director of African Studies at Northwestern University, Professor of Public Administration at Ahmadu Bello University (Zaria, Nigeria), and Dean, Faculty of Social and Management Sciences at Bayero University (Kano, Nigeria).

His numerous publications include *Religion and Political Culture in Kano* (winner of the Herskovits Prize); *The African Experience* (four volumes); *Black Africa: A Comparative Handbook*; *Social Change and Nation Building in Africa*; *Values, Identities and National Integration: Empirical Research in Africa*; and *Ahmadu Bello, Sardauna of Sokoto: Values and Leadership in Nigeria*. His most recent book is *Muslim Civic Cultures and Conflict Resolution: The Challenge of Democratic Federalism in Nigeria* (Brookings Institution Press, 2005).

He served as an international observer during the Nigerian presidential elections in 1999 (Kaduna), 2003 (Kano), and 2007 (Katsina). He was part of a team that helped plan the new Nigerian federal capital at Abuja in the late 1970s. From 1981 to 1996, he served on the executive committee of a U.S.-China scholars exchange program to help set up African studies in China. He has served on review panels at the United States Institute of Peace and participated in Nigeria working groups at the Council on Foreign Relations and the Center for Strategic and International Studies. Between 2002 and 2006, he was a member of the Brookings Institution task force on U.S. policy toward the Islamic world.

About the Institute

The United States Institute of Peace is an independent, nonpartisan, national institution established and funded by Congress. Its goals are to help prevent and resolve violent conflicts, promote post-conflict stability and development, and increase peacebuilding capacity, tools, and intellectual capital worldwide. The Institute does this by empowering others with knowledge, skills, and resources, as well as by directly engaging in peacebuilding efforts around the globe.

Faith and Politics in Nigeria

Text: Palatino and Optima

Display Text: Cochin and ITS Symbol Std

Cover Design: Hasten Design Studio and Katharine Moore

Interior Design and Page Makeup: Katharine Moore

Developmental Editor: Kurt Volkan

Proofreading: Amy Thompson

Indexing: Mary Coe

Copyediting: Janet Walker

Pivotal States in the Muslim World

As part of its Muslim World Initiative, the United States Institute of Peace's Center for Conflict Analysis and Prevention is undertaking a major analytical effort in which leading scholars and area specialists measure the influence of certain pivotal states on the broader Muslim world and assess how their political and social evolution will affect U.S. interests across the Muslim world.

This collective initiative builds on the argument put forth by Robert Chase, Emily Hill, and Paul Kennedy in 1996 that the United States should prioritize the application of its limited resources and attention toward so-called pivotal states. As they argue, such states merit particular attention because they affect—both positively and negatively—not only the stability of their respective regions but also of the larger international system. Here, focusing specifically on pivotal Muslim states and U.S. interests in the Muslim world, this project aims to identify which states in the Muslim world are most influential and critical to U.S. foreign policy. The Muslim world, for purposes of this project, includes not only states with Muslim majorities (such as Pakistan, Indonesia, Iran, and Saudi Arabia) but also states with important Muslim minorities (such as India, France, Germany, and Russia).

This volume and Graham Fuller's *The New Turkish Republic: Turkey as a Pivotal State in the Muslim World* are products of this initiative.